THE BODY SHOP

book of wellbeing

☉ THE BODY SHOP

book of wellbeing

mind, body, soul

TED SMART

This edition produced for The Book People Ltd,
Hall Wood Avenue, Haydock, St Helens WA11 9UL

1 3 5 7 9 10 8 6 4 2

First published in 1998 by Ebury Press
Random House, 20 Vauxhall Bridge Road, London SW1V 2SA

Random House Australia (Pty) Limited
20 Alfred Street, Milsons Point, Sydney, New South Wales 2061, Australia

Random House New Zealand Limited
18 Poland Road, Glenfield, Auckland 10, New Zealand

Random House South Africa (Pty) Limited
Endulini, 5A Jubilee Road, Parktown 2193, South Africa

Random House Group Limited Reg. No. 954009

www.randomhouse.co.uk

A CIP catalogue record for this book is available from the British Library.

The Body Shop Editor: Tim Blanks
Project Editor: Emma Callery
Design: The Senate
Picture Research: Nadine Bazar
Special Photography: Jonathan Root and Eric Richmond

Contributors:
Vicci Bentley: Wellbeing and the power of touch
Tim Blanks: Wellbeing and the mind-body connection
Simon Brown: Wellbeing and internal fitness, shiatsu, feng shui
Bronwyn Cosgrave: Wellbeing and exercise
Nicola Graydon and Natalia O'Sullivan: Food for the soul, Wellbeing and the soul
Jennifer Wood-Allen: Wellbeing and the way you look

The Body Shop International plc http://www.the-body-shop.com

Printed and bound in Singapore by Tien Wah Press

This book is printed on paper made from 100% chlorine-free pulp.

This book is dedicated to
Jilly Forster
– a passionate, anarchic,
visionary friend of
The Body Shop.
Long may she flourish.

conte

Introduction

Imagine an individual who embodies wellbeing. Say it's you. You know yourself pretty well. You're in control. You're productive, you value yourself. You're able to love and be loved. And all the time, you're realistic about life.

Each of these qualities is a valuable goal, but how many of them do you feel you *really* embody? Wellbeing is somewhere we all want to be. It's the modern world's ultimate challenge. But there's a lot standing in the way.

We live in a world so entrenched in designer dreams and aspirations, that we are now able to fashion our minds and bodies with such precision through drugs, personal fitness trainers and cosmetic surgery. Californian fathers award their teenage daughters with the gift of a nose job, or a chin tuck, and it is possible to alter a child's height by administering human growth hormones. But for me, the most frightening aspect of all is that according to a survey in *Newsweek* magazine, 11 per cent of parents said that if they were expecting a child predisposed to obesity, they would have it aborted. But, as we approach the new millennium, it is the 'tomorrowmakers' who will have the most profound effect on our perceptions. The US government is spending $2 billion on the Human Genome Project, which aims to decipher all 100,000 human genes. Researchers probing the nature of human disease and abnormalities have already identified some 250 human genetic defects. We are leaving behind the century of physics for a new age of biology, where inner space will absorb us as much as outer space once did. But as progress teaches us more about ourselves, how much more do we really know?

The *New York Times* argued that, 'Life is special, and humans even more so, but biological machines are still machines that now can be altered, cloned and patented.' And machines are also commodities. It's no wonder that our sense of wellbeing is frequently based not on our educational or spiritual achievements but rather on our more immediately appreciable assets: appearance, good looks and fitness. Women are particularly vulnerable. On the threshold of a new millennium, many women, when asked what influences their self-esteem, will cite their body image as a prevailing factor over intelligence, a colourful history, independence and empowerment. The current generation is the most advertising-literate, media-wise, image-saturated generation there has ever been. Yet, when you consider that the average 35-year-old woman will have seen 150,000 advertisements in her lifetime, and that one fifth of the global population watch *Baywatch*, is it such a surprise that many women feel alienated from their bodies when they compare their physical reality to the idealized illusions they see in mainstream culture?

Statistics tell the tale. The US diet industry will be worth $77 billion a year by the end of the century. Over half the female population of the US buy into this industry, and a survey of ten-year-old girls in the fourth grade found that 80 per cent were also participating. Yet ironically, 98 per cent of all those using the products and services supplied by this industry fail to achieve their objectives. In other words, the products and services do not work. The diet industry, America's fifth largest, is probably one of the most successful marketing achievements in history. What it sells is self-doubt, and it has relentlessly and successfully extended its grip to the minds and bodies of millions of women all over the world.

This most definitely is not progress.

The media's obsession with women's bodies has given rise to a distinct sense of estrangement, a schism between mind, body and soul. But looking back on the 20th century, schisms seemed to define the age, which is perhaps why the new century rides in on a desire to put things back together, re-establish old connections, rebuild communities. I hear a lot of talk about an emerging integral culture, one which connects people and nature, flesh and spirit, and people and other people all around the world. Hazel Henderson, an influential economist for whom I've got a lot of time, has very pointedly predicted, 'We will not make it as a species unless we shift from the dominator to the partnership model world-wide.'

The most fundamental partnership I can think of is that between mind, body and soul. It is the essence of wellbeing. It is also The Body Shop inspiration, and therefore the inspiration for this book. A pioneer in the cosmetics industry, The Body Shop has always endorsed a holistic concept of beauty, ie that beauty has more to do with an outward expression of inner harmony than an idealized arrangement of physical features. Holism (from the Greek *holos*, whole) is based on the idea that mind and body tend towards a natural balance, a state called homeostasis. The quest for this ideal state underlies much of the information you will find in the following pages. One thing I find enthralling is how much of the data on nutrition and self-care rings true with my instincts. But *The Body Shop Book of Wellbeing* also speaks to my spirit, and it is here that I feel we have broken

new ground, by presenting a formula for wellbeing that integrates the pragmatic concerns of the flesh with the spiritual yearnings of the soul.

A challenge for the future is really about the present. The future is now, business guru Paul Hawken once said. Better to focus on the present, because that's all there is. It is a short, sharp point with particular relevance for women. While they literally carry the seeds of the future, women facilitate the present. It hardly needs repeating that, while their self-esteem suffers, society as a whole is impaired. Viewed in this light, wellbeing is much more than an abstract, elusive idea. As the root of dignity, activism and self-expression, it is actually all about freedom – the freedom to fulfil our full human potential. And as we do that, we benefit our community and society as a whole.

I hope *The Body Shop Book of Wellbeing* will inspire you to find that freedom and fulfil your own potential.

Anita Roddick

mind
body
soul

'The flesh endures the storms of the present alone, the mind those of the past and future as well as the present.'

Epicurus, c.400 BC

wellbeing and the mind-body connection

A sense of wellbeing rests on a direct and harmonious relationship between mind and body. Stress challenges that harmony. But there is the short-term stress that excites and inspires us, and the long-term stress that makes us physically and emotionally ill. The trick is to recognize and understand our responses to the pressures of modern life.

For much of the 20th century, medicine rejected the idea that the mind could influence physical wellbeing. This truth was obscured by enthusiasm for new antibiotics and drugs that addressed specific infections and diseases without paying any attention to the whole human organism. Illnesses were strictly and artificially classified as either medical or psychiatric. Perhaps we can thank stress for medicine's revived respect for whole-ism. One of the key health issues of the late 20th century, it also offers a key to a better understanding of the mind-body connection.

We understand stress to mean the mind and body's response to external or internal pressure. The word itself is derived from the Latin *stingere*, meaning 'to pull tight', which suggests the state of alertness or readiness that stress induces. Once, it was an early-warning system, the trigger for the fight-or-flight response that was primitive humankind's best friend. Under pressure, the back muscles would clench, the heart rate, blood pressure and metabolism would increase, the desire for food, sex and sleep would diminish. The brain's stress response aimed to guarantee survival in the wild. And, jokes about the urban jungle aside, that response is still basically and unfortunately the same for us.

Recent research at the US National Institute of Mental Health has shown the extent of the connection between the immune system and the brain. They are linked by a complex network that allows for fast and constant interaction. The immune system produces chemicals that signal the brain, and the brain in turn sends chemicals to control the immune system so it won't over-react to injuries and damage tissue.

Stress and immune responses are united by a key hormone – corticotropin-releasing hormone (CRH) – which is critical for the production of the immunoregulating hormone cortisol. But above a certain level, the hormones produced by the body when it is under stress can disrupt its ability to cope. A panic attack, for instance, is the brain over-reacting to physical signs of anxiety such as increased heart rate, sweaty palms and rapid, shallow breathing. The latter can cause a fall in carbon dioxide levels in the blood, which intensifies the feelings of panic. That, in turn, worsens the symptoms, which is why you may need to breathe quickly into a paper bag to reduce carbon dioxide loss.

The over-production of hormones that results from long-term exposure to stress can disrupt the normal functioning of the mind and body, leading to a gamut of symptoms, from indigestion and aching muscles to anxiety, anger and depression. There is evidence that stress affects human immune responses to viruses and bacteria and makes the body more vulnerable to infection. The discovery of the common ground between immune and stress responses may explain why patients who are susceptible to an inflammatory disease such as rheumatoid arthritis are also so prone to depression.

It all makes perfect sense. Pressure once came in short, sharp bursts – an attack from a wild animal, for example – which often inspired an immediate solution (physical action). Modern stressors are more likely to be issues such as social status, relationships and job security, just the things to ensure that exposure to stress is prolonged and therefore more dangerous. We may still feel like taking physical action – that's why exercise is often such a great stress release – but that isn't necessarily the appropriate solution to the problem.

Illness, depression, anxiety, anger – as stress responses, they're bad news. But if we look at them as signs of a communication breakdown between the immune system and the brain, we can start thinking about reopening the lines of communication. That was the principle behind the age-old notion of 'taking the cure' in an isolated retreat, a sanatorium in the mountains, perhaps, or a hot springs spa. The quiet time gave a chance for the mind and body to get reacquainted.

Today, we have access to a huge range of therapies, mental, physical and spiritual, which aim to encourage physical and mental wellbeing. You'll find many of them referred to throughout this book. As you read about them, you will become aware that in order to cope with life, it is best to be flexible. Treatments vary for each stress. Yoga and transcendental meditation are, for example, particularly effective for depression. Cognitive therapy is good for anxieties and phobias. Any technique that slows and deepens your breathing will initially help to release tension, as will posture-improving physical therapies such as the Alexander technique. But being able to relax isn't necessarily all you need to deal with stress. Often a combination of therapies is the answer: cognitive therapy, say, with some biofeedback, physical exercise and proper nutrition. Once you have discovered the therapies that most effectively treat your symptoms, you will realize there is nothing to fear. This is a truly holistic vision of wellbeing.

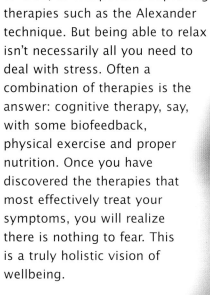

stress

■ POOR SELF-ESTEEM ■ EXPECTATIONS OF SELF AND OTHERS
■ FRUSTRATION ■ PESSIMISM ■ TIREDNESS ■ GUILT ■ MONEY
■ WORK ■ JOB INSECURITY ■ POLLUTION AND THE ENVIRONMENT
■ THE NEWS ■ SOCIAL STATUS ■ FAMILY RELATIONSHIPS ■ MARRIAGE
■ DIVORCE ■ ANXIETY ■ WEIGHT ■ LACK OF EXERCISE ■ ILLNESS ■ LOSS

Take control. Don't feel like a victim of

circumstance. If you can grasp your role

in a difficult situation, you can learn

how to resolve it.

What's the problem?

A healthy first step is to identify what is causing the stress in your life, then decide if it is avoidable. Focus on the problem, not on the feeling it leaves you with. We are all very good at training ourselves to think in certain ways. During childhood we develop certain patterns of thought and use these over and over again until, like a well-used muscle, we can automatically switch into them. Unfortunately, these can work against us. 'It's all my fault' or 'There's nothing I can do about it' signify the kind of behaviour called 'learned helplessness'. But the worst thing is to feel you are a victim of circumstance. When you feel in control of a situation you are more likely to deal with it without feeling stressed.

It is therefore important that you feel you can understand your role in why the situation arose and what you can do to resolve it. For example, if you are rejected by someone, whether in romance or in your career, try to see whether there was anything you could have done differently that would have changed the outcome, rather than see yourself as a victim. Is there something you can change about yourself that would make other people respond differently? Learn from each experience and cultivate the belief in yourself that next time you can do things differently and be more successful. In this way, you will look forward to the next experience so that you can test your new way of doing things.

The way we interact with other people has an enormous impact on our wellbeing, especially now that we know how stress affects hormonal, and in turn immune, responses. For example, women tend to feel the greatest amount of stress in a relationship that is breaking down, so the immune responses in unhappily married or divorcing women are reduced, leaving them open to illness. On the other hand, a supportive social network can boost immune response and resistance to disease, even cancer. Women with breast cancer, for instance, who receive a lot of positive support from friends and relatives during their illness have significantly longer life spans than women without such support. On a more mundane, everyday level, it is important to appreciate that other people have their own problems and the way they treat you may simply be a reflection of their own insecurities, frustrations and disappointments in life and little to do with you.

Therapies for the mind

Hypnotherapy

Hypnotherapy's benefits are well-documented. It is an excellent therapy for promoting relaxation, releasing tension and increasing self-confidence which makes it useful in the treatment of conditions such as ulcers, migraine, insomnia, asthma and high blood pressure.

On another level, as an accessible illustration of the power of the mind over the body, it makes an equally good introduction to other, more complex, forms of mind therapy.

Hypnotherapy evolved out of the work of Austrian physician Franz Mesmer at the end of the 18th century. French physicians Auguste Ambroise Liébault

and Hippolyte Bernheim raised its profile in the 19th century to the point where they received endorsements from sources as diverse as the British Medical Association and Sigmund Freud, but as medicine began to separate body and mind, hypnotherapy fell from favour. Its modern form was developed in the 1950s and 1960s by US psychotherapist Milton Erickson.

Hypnotherapy can be used in two ways. The therapist may put you in a trance and suggest that physical or emotional symptoms will disappear. Or he may use the trance state to facilitate whatever form of psychological treatment is being used. Only under the guidance of a therapist can you learn to hypnotize yourself. Auto-hypnosis has proved particularly effective in the treatment of asthma.

Australian psychiatrist Ainslie Meares has called hypnosis 'atavisic regression'. It temporarily bypasses the rational side of the brain in favour of the subconcious, liberating the instinct and helping the body heal itself. That may explain its effectiveness in treating allergies and addictions. The obvious question is whether it is removing causes or merely suppressing symptoms. A good hypnotherapist will tell you that relief of symptoms is temporary. To address causes, you will possibly need another, more intensive psychotherapy.

Autogenics

Autogenics is a series of six silent verbal exercises designed to switch off the body's stress response and switch on its relaxation response. It shares hypnotherapy's roots in the faith that the body has reserves of health-giving energy that can be liberated by autosuggestion. Among the London Centre for Autogenic Training's list of things autogenics has effectively treated are: insomnia, anxiety, migraine, high blood pressure, asthma, substance abuse, PMT and menopause.

Although autogenics was actually developed in the 1920s by Johannes Schultz, a Berlin neurologist and psychiatrist, its real guru was French pharmacist Emile Coué. He decided that it was the human imagination, not the human will, that was the reason for hypnotherapy's success. After all, you couldn't will yourself to salivate, but you could make yourself drool by imagining your favourite food. Likewise, you could imagine yourself getting better. And, drawing on the Hindu form of meditation, Coué's mantra was, in fact, 'Every day, in every way, I am getting better and better', repetition of which was designed to

induce his ideal state of 'passive concentration', where the mind would be at peace.

As its name suggests, autogenics 'comes from within'. The six exercises consist of repeated set phrases which aim to promote relaxation in different parts of the body – neck and shoulders, limbs, heart, lungs, stomach and forehead. The practitioner may, for example, ask you to repeat that your arms are heavy or your forehead is cool. Practice for about 15 minutes three times a day makes perfect.

Autogenics is usually taught in eight 90-minute sessions, though it is also possible to teach yourself. It can then be used anywhere at any time. A word of warning: once 'passive concentration', the state of deep relaxation, has been learned, it can suddenly release emotions that may have been buried. These are called 'autogenic discharges'.

Visualization therapy

Visualization therapy also harnesses the power of the imagination to fight illness, boost confidence and ease stress. It was devised by American radiotherapist Carl Simonton, whose work with cancer patients convinced him that personality was a major factor in the development of the illness. He felt it should be possible to reverse the process, and use the mind to heal rather than harm.

The therapy uses relaxation and positive mental imagery, guided by the practitioner (hence the concept 'guided imagery'). It encourages activity in the brain's right hemisphere, which governs emotions and creativity. Say you want to control your stress levels: the practitioner will help you imagine a restful scene, then focus on that scene – such as lying on a beach, feeling the sun on your skin, listening to the lapping of the waves, smelling the salt of the sea – to the exclusion of any thoughts that might distract you. The practitioner may also have you repeat positive mantra-like statements, 'I feel calm', for instance. With constant repetition, the theory goes, you will eventually come to think of the scene as real. With daily practice, you can perfect the technique so you can do it on your own.

Visualization is often used as part of psychotherapy or hypnotherapy. The kind of image the practitioner helps you form will be determined by what you hope to achieve out of your therapy. For example, if you are anxious about an illness, you may be asked to visualize locking it away in a box. Or if you are lacking in self-confidence, your therapist may ask you to visualize yourself effectively communicating with a roomful of people who applaud when you are through.

Meditation

Meditation uses a rhythmic activity (repetition of a mantra, breath awareness, t'ai chi) to focus the mind, lifting you out of your ordinary level of consciousness into a state of 'passive awareness' where the body can deal with problems such as anxiety, insomnia, high blood pressure and chronic pain.

On the Indian subcontinent and in many parts of Asia, meditation is as old as recorded history. It probably evolved from the efforts of shamans and witch doctors to enter trance states to commune with their gods. Initially, this may have meant staring at an object until the consciousness was loosed (similar to hypnosis), but eventually mantras (sacred words) were used to clear the mind.

Imagine a restful scene, then focus on that scene – such as walking on a beach, listening to the lapping of the waves, smelling the salt of the sea...

In the Buddhist East, the practice of meditation evolved into yoga, and it became the determining feature of the yogi's way of life. Meanwhile, in the Christian West, meditation became prayer, less a technique for relaxation and clearing the mind than a way of communicating with God. So meditation techniques straddled the realms of the physical and spiritual.

Western society was awakened to the potential of meditation as a physically and spiritually uplifting type of therapy in the 1960s when transcendental meditation (TM), a technique developed by a Hindu yogi named Maharishi Mahesh, attracted the attention of celebrities such as The Beatles. TM was accessible to pop stars on a spiritual quest and harried office workers alike. In the 1960s, it was proved to be a highly effective form of therapy by Dr Herbert Benson and his colleagues at Harvard University who adapted it as the basis of a best-selling book *The Relaxation Response.*

Physical and spiritual refreshment doesn't come much simpler than the basic mantra technique employed by TM: sit for 15 or 20 minutes each morning and evening silently repeating your mantra (given to you by a TM trainer) over and over.

As with the various forms of psychotherapy, there is likely to be one form of meditation you are most compatible with. It need not necessarily be the first one you come across. The best way to learn about meditation is to join a local group, especially one a friend has recommended.

Whatever the method you choose, there are some simple guidelines, which help promote relaxation:

Plan the sessions so you will not be meditating immediately after a meal or after taking stimulants.

Avoid distractions – use a quiet room and make sure you silence the telephone.

Meditate in subdued light, seated in front of a pleasant object (flowers in a vase, for instance).

Sit in a comfortable position and do whatever you need to stay that way.

If interrupted, surface slowly from your meditation. After it ends, allow a few minutes to return to the everyday world.

stress

If we look at stress responses as signs of a communication breakdown between the immune system and the brain, we can start thinking about reopening the lines of communication.

power

As an accessible illustration of the power of the mind over the body, hypnotherapy makes an equally good introduction to other, more complex forms of mind therapy.

therapy

Most methods of psychotherapy depend on a relationship of absolute trust and confidentiality between patient and therapist. This relationship aims to reflect the patient's previous significant relationships and emotions.

thought

There are many ways to change your patterns of thought. One way is to imagine a situation that you would normally find stressful and itemize your reactions.

victim

The worst thing is to feel you are a victim of circumstance. When you feel more in control of a situation, you are more likely to deal with it without feeling stressed.

Biofeedback

Biofeedback training is an increasingly popular method of stress management. You are taught by a practitioner to use information about a body function related to stress – such as blood pressure, sweating, pulse rate and muscle tension – so you can learn to control it, bringing your own blood pressure and heart rate down. Bodily processes that were once assumed to be involuntary are now recognized as controllable, which is quite a breakthrough.

Your 'teacher' is a machine to which the practitioner attaches you by a set of electrodes or probes. You are fed back information about your stress responses via flashing lights or beeps which intensify or diminish according to rising or falling stress levels, so you become aware of how you feel about stressful situations as the signals change. Then you can learn to manipulate those signals by controlling the corresponding body function with relaxation techniques (breathing, for example).

Say you had a tension headache. Electrodes would be attached to your forehead so that any movement in the muscle would be electronically detected and fed back as a beep. The tone would increase as the muscle contracted and decrease as it relaxed. By controlling the tone, you would learn to keep the muscle relaxed. The knock-on effect would be enhanced relaxation of scalp and neck muscles as well. And you would also have been made aware that, just as it was your own thought processes causing your discomfort, it was within your power to ease it.

The aim of biofeedback training is that, after four to eight weeks, you are able to regulate your stress responses without the machine. Continued advances in computer technology mean there is now interactive software to aid self-regulation.

Psychotherapy

Psychotherapy offers a number of techniques, both complex and simple, to treat psychological problems such as anxiety, phobias and personality disorders and to find effective, long-lasting ways of dealing with stress.

Most methods of psychotherapy depend on a relationship of absolute trust and confidentiality between patient and therapist. This relationship aims to reflect the patient's

previous significant relationships and emotions, which are 'transferred' onto the therapist, in theory encouraging long-suppressed motives and repressed feelings to surface.

It was Sigmund Freud who introduced the idea of the unconscious mind in Vienna at the turn of the century. His followers believe that wellbeing is conditional on an individual's 'analysis' and understanding of what makes him or her tick. Reactions, pro and con, to Freud's theories have shaped the evolution of psychotherapy. Behavioural therapists, for instance, dispute the emphasis on the unconscious and believe that behaviour can be conditioned by biological imperatives such as hunger. And Freud's own form of psychoanalysis was subverted by a breakaway disciple named Carl Jung who developed the theory of the 'collective unconscious', an inner world of wholeness that united all humankind. This world was the wellspring of myths and dreams. Jungian thought has had a major cultural influence on the late 20th century through the popular work of acolytes such as Joseph Campbell.

Also increasingly popular at the century's end is the branch of psychotherapy called humanistic therapies, the 'touchy-feely' therapies that emphasize personal growth by reinforcing an individual's positive aspects rather than delving into dysfunction. Psychosynthesis, for example, aims to help you explore and appreciate different facets of your personality through painting, movement, writing and other aesthetic activities. It is not only a way of

Choosing a psychotherapist
It can be hard choosing a psychotherapist, particularly because many practitioners use more than one kind of therapy in their treatments. The best guide is to be focused on what you want to change about yourself. Then any therapist you consult will be able to determine whether his or her technique is suitable. It pays to shop around. You may find it is a physical – rather than a mind – therapy you need.

Often you will find the initial consultation is free. It is important that you feel you can be utterly open with your therapist. If you don't feel that initial bond, it may be advisable to try another one.

See the Useful addresses at the back of the book for more information.

exploring your possibly neglected spiritual side. It also means that the more you are involved in things that enjoyably stretch you, the more confident and in control of your life you will feel.

Psychotherapeutic terms such as 'the inner child', 're-birthing' and 'the primal scream' have entered the modern vocabulary, as have the concepts of child therapy, group therapy, family therapy and marriage counselling.

Counselling itself focuses on immediate ways to boost your ability to deal with a specific problem, the loss of a loved one or a job, for instance.

Cognitive therapy

Cognitive therapy aims to change dysfunctional thinking into positive thinking by addressing the root causes of psychological problems. If you habitually respond to situations in a negative or self-denigrating way, cognitive therapy can help you learn to recognize your automatic negative thoughts and challenge them with positive evidence to the contrary.

This positivity makes for a particularly effective form of treatment for depression and phobias. One cognitive technique to deal with phobias is systematic desensitization. Rank your fears in a hierarchy, with the worst at the top, the least significant at the

bottom. Visualize the least till you no longer fear it, then do the same step by step until you reach the top of the ladder (see the exercise, opposite).

A promising footnote: now that the age of computerized self-help is upon us, researchers at the UK's Institute of Psychiatry have found a way to make cognitive therapy available without the therapist. They have come up with a CD-ROM that is called *Beating the Blues*, which helps you evaluate thoughts and feelings and monitor your behaviour yourself.

Positive associations

These can be subtle medicine. Say you were given chocolate as a reward for being good when you were a child. After a while you would associate chocolate with success. When you were feeling low, you might eat it to remind yourself of the times when you felt appreciated and loved. You can use this same process to help deal with stress. The idea is to do something while you are relaxed and happy that you can repeat when you feel stressed to trigger your relaxed state.

When you feel relaxed, press the acupressure point on the palm of your hand (see page 167). Once you have built up an association with pressing this point and feeling relaxed, you can press the point to help relax in a stressful situation.

A cognitive self-help exercise

When faced with a deadline, do you automatically begin to wonder what will happen and who you'll let down if you don't meet it? Or do you see it as an opportunity to prove yourself so you'll focus all your energy on meeting it? Now ask yourself if your answer suggests a habitual pattern of thought that helps you succeed in life. If not, it is possible to retrain yourself to think in another way. There are many ways to change your patterns of thought. One way is to imagine a situation that you would normally find stressful and to itemize your reactions. Asking for a promotion, for example. Is this your train of thought?

➊ **I will not be accepted.**
➋ **I will feel a failure.**
➌ **My colleagues will find out and talk about me.**
➍ **It will be harder to get a promotion later.**
➎ **I will feel rejected and be less happy at work.**

Now imagine another, less stressful train of thought:

➊ **I have nothing to lose.**
➋ **At least everyone will know I am ambitious.**
➌ **If I do not ask, I am less likely to get a promotion.**
➍ **It will be good practice for me.**
➎ **If I do not get the promotion, I will find out why and that will improve my chances next time.**

Some people will be good at visualizing, talking through or imagining the feelings of the process of going for the promotion. If you are naturally good at visualization, focus on how you would look, the expression on your interviewer's face as you respond and how everything would look once you succeed. If you are better at talking things through, have imaginary conversations with your interviewer. Talk your new pattern of thinking through. If you are feelings-oriented, you will find it easier to feel the confidence, power and warmth as you think through the new pattern. You may also be able to use a combination of the three.

Keep running through the thought process to train your brain to think differently. Once you feel ready, put yourself into a situation where you can use the re-training in real life. Use each situation purely for practice. Do not worry about succeeding. The more you practise, the stronger your new thought process will become.

Music and art therapy

Music *does* soothe the savage breast. Its rhythms affect heart-rate and breathing, and prompt the release of endorphins, the body's own painkillers.

Music and art both offer obvious opportunities for the release of stress and emotions, especially for people who have difficulty expressing themselves verbally. So it follows that they also make good therapy tools, whether as a self-help technique or in a more structured environment.

Splashing paint on paper or banging a drum can be useful channels for the destructive impulses that often rise to the surface before the more positive benefits of treatment emerge. This makes music and art therapy effective for a wide range of emotional and psychological disturbances, including learning difficulties, eating disorders and alcohol and drug abuse.

Sound therapy

Sound therapists believe that the body's organs and cells vibrate at specific frequencies, just like sound waves. Any disturbance of the inner rhythms is symptomatic of illness, so sound therapy aims to restore harmony, and therefore wellbeing.

Chanting is probably the most familiar example of the harmonious power of sound, but sound therapists also use a variety of other techniques to promote the body's self-healing processes:

- With cymatics, a machine transmits sound waves through the skin to a specific problem area, causing the cells to vibrate at a healthy resonance.
- Auditory integration training and the Tomatis method use machines developed by French ear specialists to retrain patients to hear and listen properly.
- Physio-acoustic methodology uses computer-generated sound waves to lower blood pressure and relax muscles.

Laughter therapy

Laughter relaxes tense muscles, eases tiredness and stimulates circulation. It even helps fight off infection and viruses by raising levels of immunoglobin A in the blood, which helps promote the activity of the white blood cells that are part of the body's natural defence system.

Who would have thought that a reaction which is so universal could pack such a positive punch? In its own small gleeful way, the fall-out from a hearty laugh is a perfect illustration of the mind-body connection we've been covering. And it's probably one of the best illustrations of an elementary principle of wellbeing: if it *feels* good, it will *be* good for you.

mind body soul

'The human body is the best picture of the human soul.'
Ludwig Wittgenstein, 1953

wellbeing and internal fitness

Diet is an ambiguous tool, too complex and emotionally charged to be prescribed lightly, yet too powerful to be ignored.

Steven Bratman, MD

Traditionally, human beings ate foods grown locally, that had matured with and absorbed the same energy as they themselves had. Someone living in a cold northern climate would have been living on foods that were also able to cope with that climate, the theory being that if carrots, cabbages and onions could survive freezing conditions, they would have the right energy to help you cope with the same environment.

Equally traditionally, people had to eat the foods that were in season, which meant that fruit and fresh vegetables were more common during the warmer months while rich warming stews and pickles were eaten during the colder months, in northern climes at least. In hindsight, this was a naturally effective way of adjusting the body to suit the changes in the seasons.

The traditional diet was primarily grains and vegetables supplemented with fish, dairy food and meat. Although life and living conditions were hard for many people, they managed to maintain reasonable levels of health despite a lack of modern health care. And looking around the world today, those societies that still retain a traditional approach to diet, such as the Chinese, enjoy the lowest incidence of cancer, heart disease and other degenerative illnesses.

The risk of moving from a traditional to a modern diet is obvious: people become further removed from nature and lose their vital connection with the source of life.

dependency

By eating foods from all over the planet, regardless of the seasons, we have become more dependent on artificial support systems, whether from nutritional supplements, medicines or an artificial environment.

change

The food we eat has changed dramatically in the last thirty years. Fresh home-cooked foods have been replaced by pre-cooked, dried, tinned, frozen or microwaved foods. The consumption of sugar, meat and processed food has increased. Additives, nuclear irradiation and genetic engineering are changing the very nature of many foods.

toxicity

In parallel, farming methods have changed. Animals are fed with processed foods, antibiotics and growth hormones before being slaughtered for human consumption. Pesticides, chemical fertilizers and factory farming have allowed a cocktail of toxic pollutants into the food chain.

artificiality

The further we move into a world of artificial surroundings, processed foods and a sedentary lifestyle, the more stretched is the umbilical cord that connects us to the source of life. One day it may snap. Then there is no way back.

So what can we do to strengthen the connection? The experience of other societies that enjoy good health isn't as relevant as it might seem. For example, the Indian diet of grains, vegetables and pulses is very healthy, but its use of strong spices is designed to help people stay cool in a very hot part of the world. The spices help move heat from deep inside the body to the surface where it can be expelled. Eating strong curries on a regular basis would not be helpful in a cold, wet country such as Britain. Still, the one thing we can be sure of is that the food we eat is the single greatest influence on our wellbeing. Biology, history and common sense tell us that changes in the food a species lives off will eventually alter it. Is the modern Western diet giving us greater health, energy, stamina and endurance while making us more intelligent and more alert? Early indications are that it is not.

One of the problems when trying to look at modern research on diet and health is that much of it only shows you a small part of the whole picture, which can be misleading. At the same time this kind of research is often unreliable and the results can be contradictory. Some research is sponsored by food companies with a vested interest in proving that their own product is healthy. Although a food can be proved to be healthy in isolation for one type of ailment, it is not always a healthy part of a complete diet and the research can ignore other potentially harmful side effects. Even research conducted by government agencies is vulnerable to lobbying and interference from the farming and food industries. Sources for this chapter include the World Health Organization, the Ministry of Agriculture, Fisheries and Food and the Medical Research Council in the UK; and Cornell University and the Department of Agriculture in the US, which will hopefully provide a balanced view.

In the largest-ever study on diet and health, a team of international researchers acting under the auspices of Cornell University in 1990 examined the diet of 6,500 people in China and ran numerous tests to measure the effect on their health. The China Health Project has radically changed thinking on many aspects of nutrition. One of the findings was that weight is primarily determined by intake of saturated fat rather than calories. The Chinese in the study ate 20 per cent more calories, twice as much starch, but only one third of the fat found in the American diet. Yet the study found that Americans were on average 25 per cent fatter than the Chinese, even taking into account their different heights. This would suggest that the best way to lose weight is to cut fat, not calories.

Other surprising results were that eating dairy foods could actually increase the risk of weaker bones and, contrary to popular sentiment in the West, vegetarians had excellent iron counts. In fact, the controversial conclusion of the China Health Project was that human beings are essentially a vegetarian species.

Diet and digestion

Understand how your digestive system works, keep it in good condition, and you can prevent the illnesses that may arise in this part of your body.

The digestive system breaks down food and readies it for absorption. So the type of food you eat will affect the internal environment of your stomach, intestines and bowels. Common acid-forming foods include coffee, sugar, citrus fruits and wine. They create a condition in your stomach that can lead to indigestion. Foods such as meat create a more acidic condition as they require you to secrete stronger acids to aid digestion. Stress also makes your body secrete more acid into the digestive system, which accounts for the gnawing feeling in your stomach when you are tense.

As the acids are absorbed, your blood normally becomes more acidic. If it is too acidic to begin with, various health problems can arise, including indigestion, headaches, cystitis and difficulty in relaxing. And if over-acidity is allowed to persist, you will be more predisposed to rheumatoid arthritis, stomach ulcers and cancer.

Reducing the amount of acid-forming foods in your diet can help reduce the acidity of your blood. Increasing the quantity of grains, vegetables and beans can help make your blood more alkaline. The Japanese use a special pickled plum called an umeboshi with bancha twig tea to make a drink designed to reduce acidity. Umeboshi plums and bancha twig tea are available in health food shops. Simply place half a plum in a cup, fill with hot bancha tea and stir. As well as reducing acidity in the stomach, this drink eases indigestion and helps prevent a hangover.

A diet high in saturated fats, such as meat, eggs and cheese, will tend to slow down food moving through your digestive system. It normally takes high fibre foods between 12 and 24 hours to pass through your intestines, but meat typically takes 48 hours. And in an elderly person, it can take up to two weeks.

To test your own intestines, eat lightly cooked or raw corn on the cob. Try to swallow the kernels whole. You will be able to see them in your following bowel movement. Measure the time from eating the corn to your bowel movement to see how well your intestines are working. Most common problems arise from the intestines being too slow. One of the risks is that toxins develop as faecal matter decays. These are absorbed into your blood. A diet high in fibrous foods such as brown rice, pasta, couscous, bread, vegetables and fruit will help maintain a healthy digestive system.

Studies in Britain found that at least 37 g of fibre is required per day to achieve a healthy intestine and regular bowel movement. For example, in an average daily intake of 1500 g of food, every 100 g should contain at least 2.5 g of fibre.

Fibre content measured in grams per 100 grams (g/100 g)

Grains
Brown rice (boiled)	1.5
Corn on the cob (boiled)	4.7
Oatmeal (porridge)	0.8
Wholemeal flour	9.6
Wholemeal bread	8.5

Vegetables
Broccoli tops (boiled)	4.1
Brussels sprouts (boiled)	2.9
Cabbage (raw)	3.4
Carrots	3.1
Leeks (boiled)	3.9
Onions	1.3
Parsley (raw)	9.1

Beans
Butter beans (boiled)	5.1
Chickpeas (boiled)	6.0
Lentils (boiled)	3.7
Split peas (boiled)	5.1

Fruit
Apples (raw)	2.0 (Peel 3.7)
Peaches (steamed)	5.3
Raisins (dried)	6.8

Meat
Chicken	None
Fish	None
Dairy foods	None
Eggs	None

Source: The Composition of Foods. Ministry of Agriculture, Fisheries and Food, and Medical Research Council (published by HMSO, 1988), and US Department of Agriculture, Handbook No. 456.

The type of food you eat will influence the quality of your blood in ways other than extra acid. Eating fattier foods creates a condition where the haemoglobin sticks together, effectively reducing the surface area available to absorb oxygen. This means that, for each breath of air, the blood absorbs less oxygen as it circulates through the lungs, resulting in shortness of breath and less than optimum fitness.

The balance of acid, alkali, sodium and potassium in your blood will also affect its quality. Extremes of either of these can lead to poor health, most often resulting in high blood pressure. The World Health Organization links high blood pressure with increased risk of strokes and coronary heart disease. To diminish the risk, you should eat a diet low in fat and high in complex carbohydrates, which are found in grains, vegetables and beans. In addition, reduce intake of alcohol and salt. And using processed low-fat alternatives can be just as harmful as the traditional sources of saturated fat. It is not clear that eating margarine is any more healthy than butter. But there are alternatives such as tahini and hummus that have been used safely for hundreds of years.

Foods containing refined sugars – sweets, cakes and convenience foods – place more extreme demands on your body. As refined sugar is a single molecule (monosaccharide), it is quickly absorbed through the tongue and stomach so it results in a sudden rise in blood sugar levels. Your pancreas has to secrete insulin to get your muscles to absorb sugars from your blood. Typically, your blood sugar will then fall to a level lower than before you ate the sugary food. If you are eating sugary foods throughout the day, your blood sugar levels are likely to seesaw, leading to mood swings and changes in your energy levels. In extreme cases, people become tired, shaky and irritable as their blood sugar reaches its lowest point, which will sabotage any attempt at wellbeing. Worse, over time, this process can have an adverse effect on your pancreas, eventually leading to diabetes.

What is going on inside?

Once it has affected your blood, the food you eat will then affect the condition of your organs, as the blood travels through them.

Bones

Osteoporosis is a condition where bones lose their density, becoming brittle and weak. It is claimed that 25 per cent of sixty-five-year-old American women have lost 50 per cent of their bone density. One of the surprise findings of Cornell University's research into the health of people living in rural China in 1990 was that osteoporosis was uncommon among Chinese women even though they consumed only half the calcium typical of an American diet. Amazingly, five separate studies found that even though someone may have an adequate supply of calcium, they actually lose calcium from their bodies if they also eat a protein-rich diet. The conclusion is that if your source of calcium during adulthood is mainly from milk, cheese and yoghurt, you may end up losing more calcium than you take in.

Liver and gall bladder

The liver produces bile to digest fats. It is then stored in the gall bladder. But stones can form in the gall bladder, leading to a sharp pain each time it contracts to excrete bile. The World Health Organization (WHO) research in 1990 noted that gallstones are a greater problem in countries that eat large quantities of saturated fats, and that in these countries vegetarians have a lower incidence of gallstones.

Breasts

Again, fats from meat and dairy food seem to be one of the main causes of breast cancer. By comparing different diets and death rates from cancer around the world, the WHO found a direct link between the levels of fat in a diet and the risk of breast cancer. Research has shown that women eating meat daily are four times more likely to develop breast cancer than those who eat little or no meat. Similar results were found with eggs, butter and cheese. It has also been found that women whose diet is high in fats and protein reach menopause at an average age of fifty, whereas those eating few or no animal fats begin at an average age of forty-six. The later menopause begins, the greater is the risk of breast cancer.

Heart

Blood that is rich in fats increases the risk of hardened, clogged arteries which strain the heart, leading, in extreme cases, to coronary disease. It is now thought

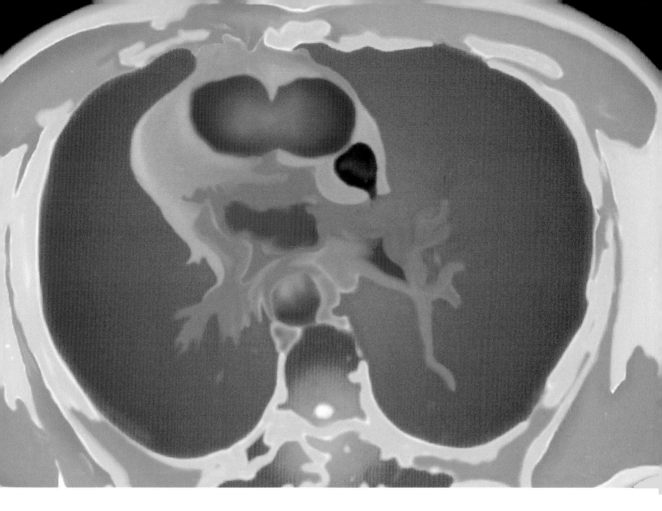

that a diet with less than 10 per cent fat and with appropriate exercise can actually reverse this process. The WHO research found that for people living in rural China the incidence of coronary heart disease is only 4 per cent of that found in Great Britain. They noted that once saturated fat intake exceeds 10 per cent of an individual's energy intake, there is a marked increase in the risk that they will die from coronary heart disease. The WHO also found that British vegetarians have a 30 per cent lower rate of coronary heart disease mortality than non-vegetarians. They discovered that cholesterol levels were lowest in people eating a vegan diet, which excludes meat and dairy food.

Lungs

Fatty foods are often associated with allergies and asthma. Researchers in Sweden found dramatic improvements when asthma sufferers eliminated meats, eggs and dairy food from their diets. And the *Journal of the American Medical Association* reported that vegetarians have distinctly lower rates of lung cancer. According to research by J. Strawler, elevated cholesterol, caused by saturated fats, may increase the risk of lung cancer in smokers.

Nutrients

For most of the recent past, it has been widely assumed that people needed to eat meat for protein and iron, and milk for calcium. Reports from the World Health Organization and the China Health Project have changed many of these theories.

protein

Someone eating a high protein diet will lose calcium, which in turn increases the risk of kidney stones and can weaken your bones.

iron

Meat is not an essential part of the human diet. Many other foods have greater concentrates of iron.

calcium

A more than adequate amount of calcium can be absorbed from a diet containing no dairy products.

vitamin B12

The human body can store up to four years' supply of vitamin B12 in the liver.

vitamin D

In climates where there is not much sun, dietary sources of vitamin D are important.

Protein

It seems it would be almost impossible not to get enough protein as long as you eat a varied diet with normal regular meals. Any natural food will have protein or it could not grow. Nathan Pritikin, a leading nutritionist, found it impossible to design a diet with less than 9 per cent protein unless it contained a high proportion of refined sugar. In fact, the WHO recommends a minimum intake of 32 g of protein per day, or 4.5 per cent of calorific value. In the past it was claimed that meat had a higher quality of protein. Leading medical opinion no longer supports this view.

Rather than worrying about too little protein, our concern should be the damage done by too much protein. Someone eating a high protein diet will lose calcium, which increases the risk of kidney stones and can weaken their bones. Research shows that vegetarians have a much lower incidence of kidney stones than meat eaters. A good indication of nature's recommendation is to compare the protein content of human breast milk (01.3 g/100 g) with other foodstuffs.

Protein content measured in grams per 100 grams (g/100 g)

Grains	g/100 g
Brown rice (boiled)	02.6
Corn on the cob (boiled)	04.1
Oatmeal (raw)	12.4
Wholemeal flour	13.2
Wholemeal bread	08.8

Vegetables	
Broccoli tops (boiled)	03.1
Brussels sprouts (boiled)	02.8
Cabbage (raw)	02.8
Kale (boiled)	01.5
Leek (boiled)	01.8
Parsley (raw)	05.2
Peas (boiled)	05.0
Radishes (raw)	01.0
Shiitake mushrooms (boiled)	09.5
Watercress (raw)	02.9

Beans	
Butter beans (boiled)	07.1
Chickpeas (boiled)	08.0
Lentils (boiled)	07.6
Soya beans (boiled)	10.5
Split peas (boiled)	08.3

Soya products	
Miso	11.8
Tofu	07.4

Fish	
Cod (poached)	20.9
Haddock (steamed)	20.8
Herring (grilled)	20.4
Plaice (fried in bread crumbs)	18.0
Mackerel (fried)	21.5
Mussels (boiled)	17.3
Salmon (steamed)	20.1
Trout (steamed)	23.5
Whitebait (fried)	19.5

Seeds
Pumpkin	25.0
Sesame	25.0
Sunflower	21.0

Nuts
Almonds	16.9
Peanuts (roasted)	24.3
Walnuts	10.6

Fruit
Apples (raw)	00.3
Raisins (dried)	01.1

Dairy food
Butter	00.4
Cheese cheddar	26.0
Cheese cottage	13.6
Egg (boiled)	12.3
Milk fresh skimmed	03.4
Milk fresh whole	03.3
Yoghurt natural low-fat	05.0

Meat
Bacon (fried)	24.1
Beef (minced and stewed)	23.1
Beef steak (grilled)	27.3
Chicken (roasted)	24.8
Curried meat	09.6
Irish stew	05.2
Lamb chops (grilled)	23.5
Shepherd's pie	07.6

Human breast milk
Human milk, mature	01.3

Source for this chart and those on pages 54-9: The Composition of Foods. Ministry of Agriculture Fisheries and Food, and Medical Research Council (published by HMSO, 1988), and US Department of Agriculture, Handbook No. 456.

Iron

Lack of iron leads to anaemia and tiredness. The easy test is to check the colour on the inside of your lower eye lid. Gently pull the skin down. Ideally the inside should be a reddish pink. Paleness could indicate your iron levels are too low.

The China Health Project showed that meat is not an essential part of the human diet and that many other foods have greater concentrates of iron. The Department of Health estimates we require an average intake of 6.7 mg per day for an adult male and 11.4 mg per day for an adult female.

Iron content measured in milligrams per 100 grams (mg/100 g)

Grains	mg/100 g
Brown rice (boiled)	00.50
Corn on the cob (boiled)	00.90
Oatmeal (raw)	04.10
Wholemeal flour	04.00
Wholemeal bread	02.50

Vegetables	
Broccoli tops (boiled)	01.00
Brussels sprouts (boiled)	00.50
Cabbage (raw)	00.60
Kale (boiled)	00.90
Leek (boiled)	02.00
Parsley (raw)	08.00
Peas (boiled)	01.50
Radishes (raw)	01.90
Shiitake mushrooms (boiled)	00.44
Watercress (raw)	01.60

Beans

Butter beans (boiled)	01.70
Chickpeas (boiled)	03.10
Lentils (boiled)	02.40
Split peas (boiled)	01.70

Soya products

Miso	02.74
Tofu	01.20

Fish

Cod (poached)	00.30
Haddock (steamed)	00.70
Herring (grilled)	01.00
Plaice (fried in bread crumbs)	00.80
Mackerel (fried)	01.20
Mussels (boiled)	07.70
Salmon (steamed)	00.80
Trout (steamed)	01.00
Whitebait (fried)	05.10

Seeds

Pumpkin	15.00
Sesame	07.50
Sunflower	06.70

Nuts

Almonds	04.20
Peanuts (roasted)	02.00
Walnuts	02.40

Fruit

Apples (raw)	00.30
Raisins (dried)	01.60

Dairy food

Butter	00.16
Cheese cheddar	00.40
Cheese cottage	00.10
Egg (boiled)	02.00
Milk fresh skimmed	00.05
Milk fresh whole	00.50
Yoghurt natural low-fat	00.09

Meat

Bacon (fried)	01.30
Beef (minced and stewed)	03.10
Beef steak (grilled)	03.40
Chicken (roasted)	00.80
Curried meat	02.90
Irish stew	00.60
Lamb chops (grilled)	01.90
Shepherd's pie	01.10

Human breast milk

Human milk, mature	00.07

Calcium

The brittleness caused in bones and teeth by a calcium deficiency is a slow process and most likely to affect people over the age of fifty. Though it has been assumed that dairy food is the best source of calcium, the China Health Project found that a more than adequate amount of calcium can be absorbed from a diet containing no dairy products. As dairy foods tend to be high in saturated fats, it is important to know how to do without them but still eat a diet that is high in calcium. Vegetables, pulses, fish, nuts and seeds should be a more than adequate source.

Calcium content measured in milligrams per 100 grams (mg/100 g)

Grains	mg/100 g
Oat meal (raw)	053
Rye (whole germ)	038
Wholemeal bread	023

Vegetables	
Broccoli tops (boiled)	140
Chinese leaves	076
Kale (boiled)	072
Parsley (raw)	330
Watercress (raw)	220

Beans	
Chickpeas (boiled)	064
Haricot (boiled)	065
Soya (boiled)	068

Soya products	
Miso	066
Tofu	507

Fish	
Cod (poached)	029
Haddock (steamed)	055
Herring (grilled)	039
Mackerel (fried)	028
Mussels (boiled)	200
Salmon (steamed)	029
Whitebait (fried)	860

Seeds
Sesame	137
Sunflower	117

Nuts
Almonds	250
Peanuts (roasted)	061
Walnuts	061

Dairy food
Butter	015
Cheese cheddar	800
Cheese cottage	060
Egg (boiled)	059
Milk fresh skimmed	120
Milk fresh whole	120
Yoghurt natural low-fat	180

Meat
Bacon (fried)	013
Beef (minced and stewed)	018
Beef steak (grilled)	007
Chicken (roasted)	009
Curried meat	033
Irish stew	012
Lamb chops (grilled)	009
Shepherd's pie	015

Human breast milk
Human milk, mature	034

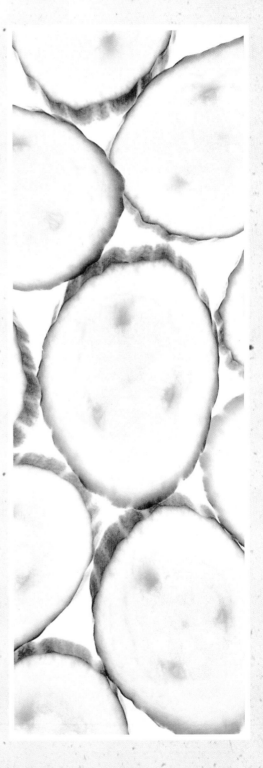

Vitamin B12

The human body requires very small amounts of vitamin B12. It can store up to four years' supply in the liver. There have been rare cases where people eating a vegan diet have suffered from low B12 levels, which can lead to pernicious anaemia if left untreated. One symptom is a general tiredness and, eventually, swelling of the joints. Children, breast-feeding mothers and pregnant women are most at risk. In traditional diets with no meat, B12 was obtained through fermented products – miso and tempeh in Japan for instance. If in doubt, fish provides relatively high concentrates of B12.

The Department of Health recommends 0.4 mg of vitamin B12 for babies rising to 1.25 mg for adults per day.

Vitamin B12 content measured in milligrams per gram (mg/gm)

Soya products	mg/gm
Miso	00.21
Tempeh	00.84

Fish	
Cod (poached)	02.00
Haddock (steamed)	01.00
Herring (grilled)	11.00
Plaice (fried in bread crumbs)	01.00
Mackerel (fried)	12.00
Oysters (raw)	15.70
Salmon (steamed)	06.00

Beers	
Strong ale	00.37
Pale ale	00.14
Draught bitter	00.17

Dairy food	
Butter	Trace
Cheese cheddar	01.50
Cheese cottage	00.50
Egg (boiled)	01.70
Milk fresh skimmed	00.30
Milk fresh whole	00.30
Yoghurt natural low-fat	Trace

Meat	
Bacon (fried)	Trace
Beef (minced and stewed)	02.00
Beef steak (grilled)	02.00
Chicken (roasted)	Trace
Curried meat	01.00
Irish stew	01.00
Lamb chops (grilled)	02.00
Shepherd's pie	01.00

Human breast milk	
Human milk, mature	Trace

Vitamin D

In many countries, sufficient vitamin D is obtained through exposure to sunlight but in a climate like the UK's, where there can be little sunlight during the winter months, dietary sources are important. The commonest symptom of a deficiency is a condition called rickets. It normally affects children, who will grow up with bowed legs as a result. Fortunately, proper nutrition and exercise can fix rickets. Fish is the healthiest source of vitamin D, although it is also found in dairy foods, eggs and liver. Those fish that are high in vitamin D are listed below.

Vitamin D content measured in milligrams per gram (mg/gm)

	mg/gm
Cod roe	02.0
Herring (grilled)	25.0
Kipper (baked)	25.0
Mackerel (fried)	21.0

Yin and yang

A yang personality: active, dynamic, focused, good with details, quick, accurate, alert, precise, interested in science, good at maths and assertive.

A yin personality: creative, artistic, sensitive, flexible, open-minded, broadminded, caring, laidback, imaginative, supple, patient, gentle, sympathetic and peaceful.

Understand the subtleties of the Oriental principles of yin and yang and you'll be better able to understand the connections between you and your environment. The weather, the phases of the moon and the seasons all affect our thoughts, emotions and behaviour. There are, for instance, more car accidents, crimes and admissions to hospital casualty wards during a full moon. For more than 4,000 years, Oriental philosophers have claimed we become more yang – aggressive and outgoing – during the full moon. Conversely, at the time of a new moon, we become more relaxed and introspective: yin attributes.

Armed with this simple piece of knowledge, you can achieve more with less effort by letting the forces of nature work for you rather than against you. Say you were planning a party, for instance. Hold it just before or on a full moon, when people are feeling more outgoing, and you'll get a big and sociable turnout. If, however, you decide to hold the party on the new moon, the risk is that less people will come and they'll be a lot quieter.

Yin and yang can be applied to all aspects of your life, from what you eat and how you exercise to the way you heal yourself. The idea is that any activity can change your own energy. In Oriental medicine, the chi energy flowing through your body carries your thoughts, emotions and ideas. Therefore you can change the way you think and feel by changing your chi energy. This partly explains why people claim to have recovered from serious illnesses simply by thinking more positively. The thoughts change the quality of chi energy which flows to every cell in your body, changing the quality of each cell. In this philosophy, every cell is fed by your thoughts and emotions.

☯ Yin and yang emotions

Though everyone will have particular strengths that will reflect one or the other, no one is entirely yin or yang. Nevertheless, your emotions and reactions to situations will change depending on whether you feel more yin or yang. This particularly applies to situations where there is no real reason to hold strong emotions. Say you wake up feeling depressed or lose your temper over something small – you can use yin and yang to change the situation.

When you are more healthily yang, you are likely to feel confident, pro-active, enthusiastic, responsible and in control of your life. If you become too yang, you can become aggressive, angry, impatient, intolerant, domineering, overbearing, violent and frustrated. To address these strong emotions, you would need to be more yin.

If you are more healthily yin you are likely to feel a sense of inner peace, relaxation, harmony and ease with other people. Should you become too yin, you could feel depressed, pessimistic, disheartened and tearful. To change this emotional state you need to be more yang.

☯ Yin and yang ailments

In the long term, being too yang will lead to stiffness, tense muscles, tightness in the abdomen, headaches at the back of your head, constipation, trouble sleeping and eventually an increased risk of clogged arteries.

Being too yin for a long time can result in feeling run down, cold, being more susceptible to infectious illnesses, poor circulation, fluid retention, low energy levels, difficulty in getting up in the morning, lethargy, headaches at the front of your head and diarrhoea.

☯ Yin, yang and diet

Where yin and yang become particularly powerful is when you wish to change something about yourself. Say you wish to be more assertive, confident and active, then you want to become more yang. You can do this by changing your diet, which

will make your blood more yang and in turn alter the way you think and feel, helping you to achieve your objectives. But if you eat a diet that is too yin, you will sabotage your attempts at self-improvement because you will feel more depressed, insecure and lethargic. The first step is to decide whether you need to be more yin or yang to achieve your aims in life or simply to feel better. Then make the appropriate changes in your diet.

The first list contains those foods that make up a healthy diet.

YANG

Sea salt
Fish
Grains – such as brown rice,
porridge, pasta, bread,
couscous, polenta,
corn on the cob
Beans
Root vegetables
Leafy green vegetables
Tofu
Nuts and seeds
Fruit
Liquids

YIN

This list contains cooking styles ranging from yang to yin. The longer food is cooked, the more yang it becomes.

YANG

Baking
Pressure cooking
Stews and casseroles
Long cooked soups
Slow boiling
Deep frying
Sautéed, Stir frying
Steaming
Blanching or quick boiling
Raw

YIN

The following is a list of less healthy foods that represent more extremes of yin and yang.

YANG

Meat
Eggs
Chicken
Hard cheeses
Soft cheeses
Butter
Milk
Yoghurt
Sugary foods
Sugary soft drinks

YIN

Your food can also be made to be more yin or yang by the way in which it is seasoned.

YANG

Sea salt
Miso
Shoyu – natural soya sauce
Ginger
Garlic
Natural vinegars – cider or rice
Fruit juices

YIN

Yin and Yang meals

The following are examples of meals that would be more yin or yang while maintaining a healthy balance.

MORE YANG

Porridge with roasted seeds
Toast with tahini or peanut butter
Steamed root vegetables dipped in hummus

Grilled fish, pasta and stir-fried vegetables
Deep fried tofu, brown rice, boiled carrots and sauerkraut
A bean and root vegetable stew on couscous with steamed greens

Miso soup with root vegetables and ginger
Noodles in broth with fish, root vegetables and lightly boiled vegetables
Steamed fish, brown rice, sautéed vegetables and steamed greens
Smoked salmon sandwiches and blanched vegetables

MORE YIN

Pancakes with sugar-free jam or pure maple syrup and lemon
Fresh fruit
Porridge cooked with raisins

Steamed tofu, couscous and a raw salad
Pasta with a pesto sauce and lightly steamed vegetables
Corn on the cob, blanched vegetables (boiled for one minute) and hummus

Watercress soup
Cucumber and shrimp bagel with pickles – sauerkraut or gherkins
Pasta salad – pasta, beans and vegetables – with smoked tofu
Polenta, sugar-free baked beans and blanched vegetables

Eating for health

It's not only what you eat but how you eat that makes you healthy. In general, there is one simple guide to good eating: the less the food has been processed, the more it benefits your body. Eating wholefoods gives you not only vitamins and minerals but phytochemicals as well. Phytochemicals have been touted as the vitamins of the 1990s. They give plants their colour, taste and natural defence against the damaging rays of the sun. Eating phytochemicals in fresh food means you reap benefits that haven't even been researched yet. The following ideas offer some other simple guidelines designed specifically for healthy eating.

Grains and vegetables

Try to eat grains and vegetables at every meal. This will ensure that you have the basic ingredients for health.

Variety

Eat a wide variety of foods to ensure your diet has all the nutrients you need and increase your ability to feel satisfied after each meal.

Ingredients

Try to select fresh organic ingredients whenever possible. This will ensure your body has the best quality fuel to give you the purest energy.

Antioxidants

The body produces free radicals, toxic molecules of oxygen, in its fight against bacteria, but these molecules also oxidize – literally rust – the body's healthy cells. They are implicated in everything from cancer to the ageing process. But you can combat free radicals with a diet rich in antioxidant nutrients. The most common are vitamins A (found as beta-carotene in carrots and broccoli), C and E, and the minerals selenium, zinc, manganese and copper. The average Western diet can be naturally low in selenium, which means this is one instance where a supplement may be valuable (vitamin E helps its absorption). And many people will undoubtedly find it reassuring that red wine is a good source of copper (which may help explain why the French have Europe's longest life expectancy).

Cooking styles

Vary cooking styles so that you have many different kinds of energy in your meals. Look at the yin and yang lists of foods on page 63 and during the course of a typical week include all these cooking styles.

Cookers

The best form of cooker is gas as your food will be prepared on a natural flame. A gas, oil, wood or coal-fired Aga will also be favourable. Electric cookers immerse food in an

electromagnetic field which can upset the chi energy of your food. A microwave cooker subjects food to an intense electrical field which disperses the chi, meaning that the feeling of wellbeing you seek from your food will be more elusive.

Drinking

It is common sense in most situations to listen to your body's needs and drink when it tells you it is thirsty. Because you absorb water from food and air, it is difficult to determine exactly how much you should drink. If you consume too much liquid, you can overwork your kidneys and increase the risk of fluid retention. As a rough guide, you should not need to get up in the night to pee.

Chewing

As you chew, you are mixing food with your saliva, which chemically breaks it down, making it easier to digest. Not only does this help avoid indigestion but it also increases your ability to absorb nutrients properly, so you feel more satisfied after a meal and your desire to snack is reduced. Try to chew each mouthful at least 30 times.

Relaxing

Relaxing and taking your time to eat will help ensure your stomach and intestines work properly. Make sure the environment is enjoyable and that you feel calm. If you feel tense, angry or

upset, take the time to calm down before eating.

Sitting

When you sit down to eat, your stomach adopts the proper shape to hold and process food. Eating on the run increases the risk of indigestion and can lead to digestive disorders.

Regular meals

Eating your meals at the same time each day sets up your biological clock so that your body prepares itself for food. This greatly reduces your desire to eat between meals, giving your intestines the chance to digest and rest, which is particularly important if you want to lose weight.

Three hours before bed

After you eat, your energy and blood concentrates around your intestines as you absorb your food. It is therefore a mistake to do strenuous exercise as it will take energy away from your intestines. Equally, it is unhealthy to sleep while you are digesting your food as the energy that should be devoted to repairing and rebuilding the cells in your body will be focused on your intestines. In addition, your digestive system is designed to work best while your torso is upright. Whenever possible, eat at least three hours before you sleep, which will help you wake up feeling refreshed and ready to start the new day.

Fasting

The idea of fasting is to rest your digestive system and give your body an opportunity to clean itself out. It needs to be done with great care to avoid weakening your energy, especially if you are involved in strenuous exercise or doing a potentially dangerous job. It is advisable to discuss your plans with your doctor before starting to fast.

For three days before you begin a fast, start to make your diet more simple. Eliminate coffee and sugar during this time so that you can gently work into your fast. Making a sudden change can cause headaches, dizziness and nausea. Likewise, all your good work will be wasted if you subsequently rush into a binge of sugary or fatty foods. So plan to ease out of your fast by eating more simple foods such as soups, grains and vegetables.

There are many types of fast some of which are given here. One of the secrets of success is to find a method that works for you.

One day a week

Set aside one day a week when you just drink water. This kind of fast is most effective if you can naturally establish a rhythm so your body expects not to eat on this day.

Grains and vegetables

The easiest fast is to eat only grains and vegetables for three days. This fast will keep a wide range of nutrients flowing into your body while still encouraging it to clean itself out.

Grains

If you wish to become more yang, try eating only grains for three days. Brown rice is the grain that would be most cleansing.

Fruits

If you wish to be more yin, try eating nothing but cooked and raw fruits. Use apples, pears, cooked raisins, peaches, apricots, grapes, tangerines, plums and berries. Too many citrus fruits can lead to over-acidity. If you feel weak or cold during the fast you are probably too yin already, in which case this fast is not right for you.

Juices

The most yin fast is to drink nothing but raw fruit and vegetable juices. Begin by only doing this for one day, then wait a week and try again.

Water

Water is the most important ingredient for survival in the short term. You need to include fresh, clean water in any fast. However, you can try consuming nothing but water for one day when you feel your digestive system needs a complete rest.

Eliminating toxins

All of us are exposed to pollutants that are toxic to our bodies. They are present in the foods we eat, the liquids we drink and the air we breathe. In the long term and in large quantities they are associated with increased risks of cancer so it is helpful to find ways to eliminate them from your body. Here are some suggestions for you to try:

Organic foods
The best way to eliminate toxins is to reduce your intake of foods that contain them. Eat organic foods whenever possible and reduce your intake of processed foods which often have additives, some of them toxic. The further down the food chain a food is, the more chance it will have greater concentrates of toxins. This is especially true of meat and dairy foods.

Seaweeds
Seaweeds can encapsulate toxins inside your blood in a way that makes it easier to eliminate them. Start with wakame, kombu and nori. Wakame is a seaweed that can be cooked in soup. Kombu is used in vegetable or bean stews and casseroles in the same way as you would use bayleaf. Nori comes in the form of a sheet of paper and is used to make sushi rolls.

Mooli radishes
In Oriental medicine, radishes in general, but particularly the long white radish called mooli, are thought to help break down fats and aid the process of cleaning your blood of toxins. Eat as a part of your regular diet, especially when you have a meal with excess fat or oil.

Sour foods
Again according to Oriental medicine, sauerkraut, gherkins, natural vinegars and lemon all stimulate the liver, which cleans the blood and helps eliminate toxins from the body.

A word of warning: while toxins are being eliminated, it is common for them to enter your bloodstream. As they pass through your brain, they can cause headaches, mood swings and fogginess, which can last up to three days.

Healing foods and natural remedies

Here are a selection of different natural remedies that are useful for everyday problems. They are generally safe to use but if you have any doubts, or especially if you are seriously ill, you should first consult someone with experience in Oriental medicine, macrobiotics or naturopathy. None of these should be used as a replacement for medical advice from your doctor.

Umeboshi plums

Use umbeboshi plums to reduce acidity in the stomach. These Japanese plums are especially useful for indigestion, hangovers and headaches at the front of your head. Eat only half of a plum at a time, and a maximum of one per day for three days.

Shoyu bancha

Can help with colds, when you have flu or if you feel run down. Put one teaspoon of shoyu (natural soya sauce), in a cup and fill with hot Japanese bancha twig tea.

Green plasters

Helpful for mild temperatures in children, itchy skin and mild burns. Place a green leaf, such as cabbage, on the affected area and hold until you feel relief. For children, hold over their forehead and use in conjunction with medical advice from your doctor.

Skin scrub

Good for blood circulation, skin metabolism, stimulating your lymph system and massaging your muscles. Soak a pure cotton small hand towel in hot water, wring it out so it is damp and hot, then fold into a tight wad and scrub your skin. If you wish to gain energy, start at your feet and work upwards. To relax, begin at your head and work to your feet.

Soaking feet

Helps relaxation, good for insomnia and reduces the need to go to the toilet in the night. Heat water to as hot as is comfortable, add one tablespoon of sea salt and soak your feet and ankles for ten minutes.

Ginger compress

Improves circulation, lower back aches and low energy levels. Grate fresh ginger until you have a small handful. Squeeze the liquid into a pot of hot water. Dip a small hand towel into the ginger water, wring out, and hold over your lower back. Do not use this compress if you are pregnant.

Parsley tea

Helps with most mild respiratory ailments, such as a deep cough, mucus or wheezing. Boil one bunch of parsley in a mug of water for ten minutes and drink the liquid before a meal.

Hot apple juice

Good to help you relax and reduce stress. Heat up one cup of apple juice and drink slowly, or pour boiling water over half a cup of apple juice.

Ginger tea

Can increase energy levels and reduce sickness for pregnant women. Grate a small dessertspoon of fresh ginger and squeeze into hot water.

Grated apple for children

Can reduce a mild temperature in young children. Grate an apple and feed your child with a teaspoon. Use in conjunction with advice from your doctor.

Salt pack

Good for diarrhoea. Heat up two mugs of sea salt in a dry pan and tip onto a tea towel. Fold the towel so the hot sea salt is safely contained within the towel. Lie on your back and hold over your abdomen. This is most effective when you place the towel directly onto your skin. It is important to take great care when handling the sea salt as it can reach high temperatures which will burn. Always test the temperature with your hand before placing the towel on your abdomen.

Parsley or watercress, dulse and pumpkin seeds

This dish is helpful if you think you need more iron or are slightly run-down. Soak a 5cm (2in) strip of dulse seaweed for 5 minutes and cut finely with a bunch of watercress or parsley. Fry in cold-pressed sesame oil for 2-3 minutes. Add half a teaspoon of shoyu (natural soy sauce) and a tablespoon of roasted pumpkin seeds. Eat daily for one week and then once or twice a week.

wellbeing and exercise

Where the mind goes, our energies follow. So believe practitioners of qi gong, the ancient Chinese healing exercise. Today, exercise embraces this age-old wisdom. Exercise is swiftly moving away from the concept of 'fitness', where participants were urged to 'go for the burn' by following the motivating philosophy of 'no pain, no gain'. Fitness is no longer a fad, it's a holistic practice. Whichever exercise you pursue – from a yoga class to a tennis match – it should involve not just your body but your mind, surroundings and circumstances. Like any other productive activity, setting goals for ourselves and maintaining a realistic outlook about our abilities and limitations are all-important when it comes time to work out. And, just like the principles of traditional Chinese medicine – which teach the importance of balancing our energy forces of yin (passive) and yang (active) (see pages 60-4) – engaging in physical activity must bring to our lives a sense of harmony, not stress.

'Exercise for yourself,' says Joanna Berry, head of Britain's National Register of Personal Trainers. 'It doesn't matter how co-ordinated, sleek or svelte someone else is.' Fitness professionals like Berry agree: exercise does not have to be done in a gym, involve wearing Lycra or a leotard and needn't be done in time to music booming from a stereo system. Such elements, she claims, intimidate more people than they motivate. 'Don't ever let exercise scare you,' she adds.

But the dangers of inactivity should. Sedentary behaviour has a negative effect on nearly every aspect of our physical and mental health. A Canadian study published in the *British Journal of Sports Medicine* in 1997 found a direct link between inactivity and the physiological signs of ageing. And the decline is more apparent in women than men. But the signs, the study claimed, could be reversed with regular physical activity.

Even moderate exercise protects the body against a slew of diseases. Another study published in the *British Medical Journal* in July 1996 notes causal association between regular physical activity and reduced rates of coronary heart disease, hypertension, non-insulin dependent diabetes, osteoporosis, colon cancer, anxiety and depression. Exercise releases endorphins – feel-good hormones – in our brain, so it is often prescribed as an antidote for depression. Exercise aids digestion and helps the lungs to function better, increasing the amount of oxygen flowing through the bloodstream, so physical and mental stamina are increased.

The great Ayurvedic physician Charaka viewed physical exercise as 'that activity of the body that is desirable and capable of bringing about stability and strength.' Exercise, Charaka believed, should be practised regularly and in the right measure. Today, fitness experts from personal trainers to doctors and government health officials agree with these Ayurvedic beliefs.

But rather than dreading a longer exercise session, draw upon Chinese wisdom – switch the mind on. If you work hard at getting your head in shape, your body will follow. Physical conditioning is best achieved if the mind within the body is in a state of total wellbeing. 'It's about balance,' says Phil Hogan, co-owner of a London health club and sports medicine centre. Hogan coaches many of his clients through regular, rigorous 50-minute aerobic workouts during which he encourages clients to spread their energy out through each session. How? Instead of switching off – diverting their attention to a TV screen or plugging into a personal stereo system, for example – participants are urged to concentrate on their physical performance and focus on raising their heart rate. The end result surprises most of Hogan's clients. 'They feel relaxed and alert instead of feeling exhausted,' he says. With regular participation, physical change and an increased sense of mental focus soon become evident.

physical

To maintain a healthy body and mind, men and women of all ages should be engaging in some sort of physical activity at least five days a week for a period of at least 30 minutes. It doesn't have to be a vigorous activity such as running or taking part in an aerobics class.

activity

The American College of Sports Medicine discovered that participating in moderate physical activity – a brisk walk, house cleaning or gardening – delivers real health benefits.

benefits

Those 30 minutes of exercise do not have to be consecutive: three ten-minute bouts of exercise a day are as beneficial as one 30-minute workout.

intensity

To lose weight or significantly improve aerobic fitness, you need to work at a higher intensity so that your body is sufficiently stimulated to help it make noticeable changes in your body weight or your aerobic endurance.

Exercise and energy

Even though today's theories on exercise are far less rigid and more progressive than a decade ago – not to mention the fact that more health and fitness information is available than ever – few of us are actually listening. Researchers at Exeter University found that exercise in the UK is on the decrease. Fewer than half of all adults are regularly active. According to the Health Education Authority, only three out of ten women participate in enough physical activity to benefit their health. And yet nine out of ten women believe that it is important to exercise regularly.

Why the decline? Largely because exercise has almost been eradicated from our daily lives. For a hundred thousand generations we were hunters and gatherers. Survival demanded continuous physical activity. We were farmers for another 500 generations and then factory workers for a fraction of that. Now we've been computerized for one single generation. The human organism still needs all that continuous physical activity but we have grown lazy with technology. Today, it's easier to send an e-mail than get up from our desk and walk to the post office.

Furthermore, long scientific studies – and the facts and figures they quote – always seem so remote and removed from personal experience. But a few startling facts should make the need to exercise more urgent. Failing to exercise is as harmful to the body as smoking half a pack of cigarettes a day. Exercise lowers the rate of breast cancer, which one in 12 British women develop. And exercisers tend to live longer. Regular workouts appear to slow the stiffening in arteries that usually accompanies ageing.

Begin to exercise and you will begin to look and feel better. The body will visibly improve. You'll likely notice a clearer complexion, shiny, healthy-looking hair, and if you suffer from PMT, an elimination of that puffy feeling around your waist, feet, face and hands. Exercise improves both the circulation of blood and fluid throughout the body. Waste and excess fluid is removed more easily from every cell. The immune system is also boosted, which protects against minor and serious illness, and your sleeping patterns should improve. Working out regularly will increase your energy levels and boost your self-esteem, two factors which science says can lead to improved sexual performance. And over time, exercise will help you maintain your ideal weight. Diet without exercise means the body burns fat less effectively. 'The body uses fewer calories for energy,' says fitness trainer Karen Voight. 'So even if you are eating the same amount of food more of it is turning to fat. An exercise programme can rebound that effect.'

Exercise with a positive plan: set a goal to learn something new. Disciplines like yoga and martial arts can offer the chance for your body to learn a new physical rhythm. And they can shed light on alternatives to Western cultural thought.

Or set a goal to meet someone new. Engage in a dance class or a team sport with an open mind and you are likely to meet new people who share a common, positive interest.

The warm-up

The following principles can and should be applied to any form of exercise, regardless of duration or intensity.

Motivation

The 1980s' fitness boom conditioned most of us to dread exercise. Indeed, if you've never exercised on your own, it may seem like a daunting process: gathering your gear in the morning, carrying a heavy bag to the office, waiting in queues for machines in the gym and then for the showers, and a late-night journey home. Surveys show that most people quit exercise not because of exertion during a workout but because of the effort involved in preparation.

Exercise should never be disruptive to your daily schedule or to any other aspect of your life, your bank balance, say, or your diet (although you should increase your intake of water to at least eight glasses per day). If you are spending undue personal time dreading or preparing for exercise, perhaps you've picked the wrong activity. Exercise should work naturally into your day and it should function, ultimately, as a release. If a heavy bag is dragging you down, a swimming costume is much lighter than a pair of trainers. So start swimming. Or, take a new look at what can add up to a fitness routine – 30 minutes spread out through a day becomes a brisk ten-minute walk to work, another ten-minute walk at lunch and then a brisk walk home. Make it a mind/body experience – while you move, focus on releasing any physical stress in your body. As you stride, introduce a mantra – a short, meaningful, statement – repeated over and over again quietly to yourself. Doing this will keep you fit and clear your head.

It takes four weeks to make something a habit in our daily lives. But psychologists believe that it takes six months of consistent exercise for fitness to become a part of your life. According to Rob Shannon, visiting lecturer in health and behavioural change at London's City University, most people give up at the three-month mark. In fact, a condition known as 'gym guilt' has been identified where a tense feeling develops after a lengthy exercise lapse delivering symptoms similar to PMT – moodiness, headaches and slight depression. Most of us have experienced these feelings to some degree: motivation is the biggest obstacle standing between individuals and their fitness goals.

Staying motivated

◎ Give yourself little choice. Invest in a series of classes at a dance studio or a yoga centre that must be used within a month.

◎ Participate in a fund-raising fitness event – a charity walk or a community cycle – where preparation is vital.

◎ Muster some moral support – join a soft ball, netball or volleyball league (where weekly participation is required).

◎ If you take up an exercise with a partner – like tennis or squash – socialize afterwards.

◎ If you choose to exercise on your own and find your motivation dwindling, make a fitness appointment with yourself and keep it. Write down in your diary a week's worth of fitness appointments. As published in Zest magazine (November 1997), researchers at the University of Calgary, Alberta, Canada found that those exercisers who kept a record of their workout time exercised more frequently than those who did not. Enough Xs on a calendar, the study found, sent lapsed exercisers back to it.

The investment of time and money often discourages people from exercising regularly. The main investment fitness actually involves is a good pair of trainers. The right shoes will ensure that you are exercising safely. And experts recommend purchasing shoes that are designed for specific sports. Go jogging in a pair of aerobic shoes, for example, and you are likely to slip and fall. Look for shoes with the appropriate soles or treads for the particular activity that you are participating in.

Investing more money in fitness – paying for the services of a trainer or a health club membership – is a personal choice. Look around for a personal trainer who suits your personality: an effective session relies on chemistry and commitment. A good personal trainer will spend time getting to know what you are all about – your lifestyle, thought processes and nutritional habits. Most personal trainers are willing to work with pairs. So if you find the cost exorbitant, bring a friend or your partner to a session. If a health club membership is one of your aims, fully investigate what a club offers, from atmosphere to equipment. And read the membership contract thoroughly before you sign away your money. If possible, before you join, make time to try out the facilities for a day. Also make sure that a club's relaxation area (sauna, steam room and complementary treatments) is as up-to-the-minute as its equipment.

Relaxation

All forms of exercise should begin with relaxation. Shutting the mind off from the events and stresses of the day will allow you to focus on what's important – an hour of personal time that benefits your mind and body. Relaxation enables you to exercise effectively and efficiently. A mind that is focused on the body will safely direct it through any workout.

Coach yourself through your own relaxation process. Lie on a comfortable mat for a while in silence. Ease tension away from your body by relaxing and then contracting all of its main muscles. Start by tilting your neck back and forth. Next, move down your body. Shrug your shoulders a few times. Tense and release your arms. Hold the tension for 5 seconds and then release. Follow the same route with your legs and your feet.

Relaxation should refresh your mind and body. If you feel tense and are unable to relax fully on your own, wind down by listening to some soft music or listen to a relaxation audio tape (available at most book shops) which will thoroughly coach you through the process.

Breathing

A good way to judge whether your body is fully relaxed is by listening to your breathing. 'Become aware of your breath,' a yoga instructor will announce at the start of a class. Yoga encourages participants to view breath as an energy source that can deliver positive, natural power. Energy flows through the body as you inhale. Focusing on the breath within your body will direct new, positive energy to areas which feel stiff and tense. Exhalation should deliver the ultimate release.

Once you become accustomed to deep breathing – becoming aware of your breath – you use more of your lungs. Oxygenated blood will pump effectively to all of the organs, revitalizing them and eliminating toxins. While you are relaxing, stretching and exercising, try not to hold your breath. Blocked breath inhibits the revitalizing benefits the body achieves through breathing and stretching.

How do you know if you are breathing correctly? At first it may be helpful to examine the procedure. Breathe in deeply through your nose, expand your diaphragm and blow out through your mouth. Ask yourself a few questions: are you using your total lung capacity? Is the upper chest moving? And, can you feel the movement in your abdomen?

Relaxing

In a quiet, draught-free room, lie on a comfortable mat on your back with your legs stretched out and arms resting gently by your sides. Close your eyes and gently take a few slow, deep breaths.

Start to ease away tension by relaxing and then contracting all of the main muscles. Begin by tilting your neck back and forth. Never push your head back so far that it becomes uncomfortable. Continue to breath slowly and deeply.

Then shrug your shoulders a few times bringing them up towards your ears and down again. Make sure your head stays flat on the mat; you are concentrating on one part of your body at a time.

Work your way down your body in the same way. Tense your arms – they will automatically be drawn in nearer to your torso – and release them a few times. Hold each tension for 5 seconds before releasing. Then do the same with your abdomen, buttocks, legs and your feet.

Breath is connected with our emotions. Tension is mainly linked with sharp, quick inhalations, holding the breath, and uneven exhalations. (Many people breathe through their mouth when stressed, which means they deprive their body of oxygen.) If your breath is even, you should feel calm and relaxed. 'Correct breathing (using the diaphragm) functions as a natural tranquillizer to the nervous system,' London-based yoga instructor and author Vimla Lalvani has said. 'The deeper you breathe, the calmer the mind becomes.'

If you concentrate on the out-breath, the in-breath should come naturally. Observe all of this for ten inhalations and exhalations.

Concentrating on your breath – before you exercise – will ensure that you are relaxing but not letting go completely. Your mind should be like your body: alert and ready for action. By focusing on the breath, any stretching and exercising that follows should do so smoothly.

Stretching

Statistics may show that fewer people are exercising today. But more people are actually stretching. Most health clubs now offer a range of stretch-derived exercise classes – yoga, Pilates, stretch and tone, and Lotte Berk (see page 99). And attendance at these classes shows that they are as popular as aerobics. Why? Stretching classes are easy to follow and can be performed by anyone, regardless of age, ability or shape. Concentration is required, but co-ordination is not really necessary. And competition is absent from stretch classes because mental focus is so important. Because it is of utmost importance to stretch the body and hold it properly, focusing your attention on someone else is practically impossible.

Stretching boosts a sluggish digestive system. Stretching postures work like an internal massage. If you've eaten a heavy meal before you begin to stretch, you will certainly become aware of it. Back bends and forward bends, for example, help to stimulate the digestive organs (opposite, top left). Often we become aware of what our bodies need to eat and drink through regular, sustained stretching.

Stretching is not complicated. Touching – or trying to touch – your toes is a simple and effective stretch (opposite, top right). So is reaching your arms up straight to the sky (opposite, bottom left) or out horizontally in front of the body (opposite, bottom right). When you first begin to stretch, you may feel as though the body is

not working hard. But an important part of stretching is mental focus, which will help you master and perform stretches to your body's potential. You should never feel pain when you stretch (nor stretch if you are injured). And stretching should be done when you are warm. If you are cold, your muscles will be stiff and forcing them puts you at risk of injury. And, beware, you may feel a few aches and pains the day after you've given the body a really good stretch. But this is likely to be positive pain – showing that your body is on its way to a new-found flexibility.

Performed in tandem with deep breathing, stretching will further energize your body. The body can reach its optimum shape, fitness experts claim, by incorporating gentle stretching techniques into an aerobic workout. If you meet someone who regularly practises stretching exercises – such as yoga or Pilates – their body has definition. It has a toned, taut, shapely form. But it's not overly muscular.

Regular stretching encourages the body to move back to its natural alignment, so the three main body weights are balanced over one another. Aerobics and other cardiovascular exercise classes may burn fat, but stretching also enables the participant to become more balanced and flexible. Yogic stretches, for example, have a positive effect on bodily functions we normally think of as involuntary – the heart rate, the metabolism and blood pressure. While aerobic exercise speeds up these processes, stretching while breathing deeply will do the opposite. At the end of a stretch workout you feel relaxed and energized.

Action

Mental and physical challenge, creative stimulation, contact with nature, filling your lungs with fresh air, energy and inner balance – these components add up to an ideal workout.

But as the proliferation of gyms demonstrates, most of us still believe that the only way to take exercise is in a stuffy, fitness equipment-filled gym. There are, however, many new, stimulating ways to exercise. If you choose to join a gym or a dance studio, use the following information as a guide to other fitness options that are available. Or break away from the gym: there are other activities through which you will reap the same benefits.

Group fitness

Cynics may claim that the aerobics boom – which started in 1968 after the American fitness guru Dr Kenneth Cooper's *Aerobics* became a best-seller – is finished. But facts tell us otherwise. Most schedules at fitness clubs are packed with aerobic exercise-based fitness classes. Participate and you are likely to notice a few changes. Just as thinking on fitness has evolved, so has the traditional approach to aerobics. The emphasis of a good aerobics class is to get fit at your own pace, rather than trying to hammer out results in a matter of weeks.

Today, more people refer to aerobics-based classes as group fitness. Movement in group fitness classes is still, like aerobics, swift and physically demanding. But more instructors are conscious of the shin splints and other injuries induced by the aerobic boom. More and more classes feature steps and movements which are uncomplicated, music that is motivating and more hands-on contact with teachers. The following ideas are new classes that offer a fun, challenging workout.

Salsaerobics

Salsaerobics merges conventional aerobics moves with music and steps from Brazilian Salsa. Recommended for extroverts as classes require swinging with a partner midway through. The twisting and turning movements make it ideal for toning up the legs, buttocks and arms.

Spinning

Just like a stimulating stationary bikeathon, spinning was invented 12 years ago by fitness guru Johnny G., who teamed up with a leading bike manufacturer to sell his trademark spinning bikes. Participants cycle against resistance and as the intensity is optional, you can progress at your own pace.

Cardio funk

An effective low-impact, muscle-toning form of aerobics, cardio funk is based on the fast-moving music and footwork of hip-hop dance. To participate effectively, the dancing takes a bit of practice.

Body sculpt/Body pump

These forms of exercise build strength and endurance. Initially conceived in New Zealand, classes incorporate hand-held weights for resistance while the body stretches, bends and steps around a dance studio. Regular participation means moving from light to heavier weights. A real fat burner, working with weights develops body tone and boosts the metabolism. And participants claim that the addition of uplifting music and the attention of an instructor make it more motivating than solo weight training.

Powerboard

A shock-absorbing, springy step lends its name to this class. Circuit training and cardiovascular exercises are performed on and around the powerboard. The board's design means that people of all weights and sizes can participate.

Kick-boxing and boxercise

Classes for these areas are increasingly popular because they provide women with two things that most feel they really need – training in self-defence and spot conditioning. Kick-boxing offers a great lower body workout. Boxercise will tone the upper body.

Skipping

This is not currently taught as an exercise class, but it soon could be. More exercise buffs are jumping high-intensity ropes in the gym – four to six bursts of three to four minute sessions (alternating the feet with each rotation of the rope). The technique has been promoted recently by the American personal trainer and author Edward Jackowski who claims that all body types can benefit. Skipping burns fat, defines muscles and diminishes cellulite. As skipping is not gym-bound, Jackowski claims it is perfect for those on the go – you can take a rope

anywhere. Beginners should start with 30-second bursts, eventually moving to four-minute sessions.

Gymnastics

Gymnastics involving a vault, beam, and asymmetric bars is being taken up by more adults, most of whom have never done it before. The warm up – forward and backward rolls, handstands, cartwheels, hand springs – may bring back childhood memories. But it's a great workout. As a total body sport, it uses all of the main muscle groups and, with practice, brings improvement in posture, flexibility and movement.

The new age of weight training

Don't think bulk or muscle mass. A healthy, firm, feminine shape is what regular weight training sessions should deliver. (Those who bulk up are lifting very heavy weights of 13.5-27 kg [30-60 lb].) Weight training offers women real benefits. From the age of approximately twenty-eight, women begin to lose muscle and, regardless of how active they are, they will go on to lose about a 225 g (½ lb) of skeletal muscle tissue each year. 'The less muscle you have, the fewer calories you will burn,' says fitness instructor and author Martica K. Heaner. The result is a lower metabolism as well as a tendency to gain weight easily.

'Aerobic work increases the metabolism temporarily,' Heaner continues. 'But it won't build enough muscle to boost it permanently. Weight training is the only way to affect muscle mass.' And studies show that if you combine weight training with aerobic activity, the body will lose more fat.

At the gym, a lot of people avoid using weight machines because they look complicated. Weights are easy to use and they can be used by anyone regardless of age or ability. Regular training with weights as light as 1 kg (2 lb) will improve muscle tone and enable the body to increase its strength ability. But beginners must always use machines while supervised by a personal trainer or a qualified gym attendant. And most are advised to start on machines rather than free weights because they help to hold you in the right position.

Once an instructor shows you how to work a weight machine, he or she should emphasize the need to move slowly. A slow pace works the total muscle, increasing its possibility for strength. Some experts advise lifting weights in 12 repetitions and counting to four in both

the up and down direction. Super Slow, a strength training method currently popular in the US, advocates lifting weights in ten seconds and lowering in five (with free weights the lowering time is ten seconds). Super Slow devotees claim this will dramatically increase muscular strength.

Weight training routines may lack the freedom and fun that cardiovascular exercise offers. But as Heaner points out, they offer an ultimately efficient workout. 'With weights, the good news is less is more,' she says. 'While you can do aerobic exercise daily, resistance exercises exhaust the muscles. They need time to recover. You can lift weights every day. But only if you don't train the same muscle group two days running. Train each muscle group no more than three times a week.'

Running

A stitch – a sharp pain in your lower gut – is not a sign to stop running. It's a signal to listen to your body. Maybe it's time to examine your technique. Few of us are born natural runners. But anyone can run – unless you're injured. Running is the easiest sport you could ever take up. There are no complicated routines to master and no equipment is involved.

But like any other sport, running and jogging involves technique. Follow it and you will avoid injury and build endurance. The upper body should be relaxed, with the shoulders eased down and back while the arms should be kept loose and low and the fists unclenched. To build up stamina, it is recommended that beginners should start off by alternating running with walking – follow two minutes of running with three minutes of walking until a steady pace of 20 minutes of continuous running is reached.

Running – and even walking – requires the proper shoes. And if you choose to run outdoors at night, take a partner or join a club (they are open to all levels) to guarantee your personal safety. Running on a treadmill will give the same results as running outdoors. If you live in a city where the pollution is bad and the streets busy, it is often the healthier and safest option. But running outdoors will deliver more of a sense of exhilaration. And the conditions – like wind and rough terrain – increase the effort expended while you run.

Walking and rambling

Power walking and even rambling (twice as popular as swimming, it's Britain's most popular sporting activity) make an effective workout if performed regularly: 30 minutes a day is recommended to see results.

Research at the University of California Medical Center proves the point. The research studied a group of obese patients who failed to lose weight by dieting but who then lost an average of 10 kg (22 lb) after they pursued a 30-minute-a-day walking programme for a year.

On wheels

Find your fitness destination. Whether it's peddling a stationary bike in a spinning class or hitting the open trails on a mountain bike, cycle-based exercises offer a total body workout.

Cycling

This sport can serve as both a pleasurable form of transportation and an effective workout (a 30-minute cycle expends approximately 360 calories). Though the cost and the type of bike you opt for are personal choices, if you are planning on hitting city streets and country trails, a mountain bike makes the best investment. The tyres are thicker and the gears flexible, making any journey safe and enjoyable. Before you spend, remember to check the following: the frame should be light, the brakes utterly effective, and the tyres should be at least 5 cm (2 in) thick. Crossing rough terrain with thick tyres is easier and safer. A tool kit will come in handy for longer cycle rides, and no matter where you cycle, a helmet is essential.

In-line skating

Commonly referred to as roller-blading, die-hard bladers claim the sport dates back to the 1700s when a Dutchman attempted to make a pair of summer ice skates with planks of wood and four spools. Modern-day blading traces its roots back to the early 1980s when two Minnesota brothers discovered in-line skates in a sporting goods shop, refined their design and used them to play off-season hockey. By the 1990s, their appeal had spread to Venice Beach, California and the cult was born.

Blading offers a low-impact, aerobic workout. It can't quite match running for an effective workout (30 minutes of running burns 450 calories, blading expends about 285), but like cycling, its appeal is both practical and pleasurable (roller blades are a great form of transportation). In addition, a good pair of roller blades costs about the same as a pair of top-of-the-line trainers. Furthermore, sophisticated design means that roller blades are both comfortable and safe (but be sure to wear a helmet, wrist guards, knee pads and elbow pads on city streets), and roller-blading isn't difficult to learn. A friend or an instructor can teach you very quickly.

The stretch revolution

At health clubs, yoga and other stretch-based exercise classes are now as popular as high-impact fitness classes. Stretching helps the participant become more balanced, toned and flexible. Stretching is a good way to get to know the body. It gradually increases muscle length and flexibility and long flexible muscles are less prone to injury.

While the popularity of stretching may be a recent phenomenon, its roots can be traced back thousands of years. Yoga, for instance, has been practised in India for at least 5,000 years. And its benefits remain unchanged. Yoga harmonizes the mind and body through exercise, breathing and meditation. It helps improve physical health and generates a sense of inner calm. Like other stretch classes, it encourages postural awareness and the gentle no-impact movements can dramatically reshape the body without straining the joints.

Stretch classes may lack the all-out sense of exuberance common to aerobics classes. The atmosphere is much calmer and most are performed without music (it is often used for meditation and relaxation at the end of a class) so the sense of your instructor is much closer. This makes it easier to develop a rapport with your teacher. An instructor with whom you feel relaxed and comfortable will make a big difference to your performance and advancement.

Any of the stretch classes described opposite will test that your body is working well and to its full potential.

Yoga

Yoga, in the Indian dialect Sanskrit, means 'union'. Yoga postures – known as asanas – unify the mind, body and breath so they work together as one. Yoga may not burn fat but it has tremendous toning power, particularly for areas such as the stomach, bottom and thighs. There are different varieties of yoga but all are united in a common purpose – to relieve tension from the body and offer deep relaxation. Increasingly popular is ashtanga vinyasa yoga, a more dynamic form of the ancient discipline, which is often referred to as power yoga.

Method Putkisto

Sometimes called Finnish Fitness, its co-creator, Helsinki-born, London-based Marja Putkisto developed this stretch and strength class in close collaboration with a sports physiotherapist and chiropractor in Finland. Six years ago she brought the now-popular method to London. Beginning with deep breathing, Method Putkisto requires the help of the instructor or a partner to move you into a series of stretch positions. The purpose of the class is to open your muscles and lengthen the spine, which will visibly improve your body's shape. Participants are often shocked as they compare the difference in the side of their body which has been stretched (it can lengthen up to an extra 5 cm [2 in]) with one which has yet to be.

Pilates

This is an exercise technique that lengthens and strengthens the muscles through a series of slow, controlled movements performed on a mat or with the help of a spring-resistant apparatus called the reformer. Exercises are centred around the abdomen which is used as an anchor from which the body can be stretched. Developed 70 years ago by Joseph Pilates, it was first taken up as a stretching technique by dancers such as Martha Graham, but it is now recommended as a way to stay fit, relieve stress and help those with a bad back.

Lotte Berk method

This form of exercise was developed by the German-born, London-based former ballet dancer Lotte Berk. Classes are set to uplifting music. Bouncing – to limber-up the body – soon moves on to a series of brisk floor and ballet barre-based stretches. The stretches are tough and to perform them well requires patience, concentration and practice. But the class moves along quickly. There is as much warmth and fun in a Lotte Berk class as there is discipline.

Martial arts

The Chinese believe that there are two types of exercise:
■ External, mainly focusing on strengthening the body (running and swimming, karate and the more physical of martial arts).
■ Internal, with gentler exercises that focus on developing internal strength so that it is possible to become healthier and calmer from within.

Most martial arts fall into the latter category. Though the term generally applies to ancient Chinese disciplines like t'ai chi and qi gong, today it's an umbrella term that applies to several international practices. To those who practice regularly, all serve the common purpose of delivering total wellness – stimulation of the body's circulation of blood, loose, limber joints and mental relaxation. Some martial arts require a partner. All can be practised practically anywhere. Performing outside on a pleasant day enables you to draw more qi from 'the great qi' – the sky. Like yoga, practitioners of martial arts claim the best way to start is by finding a good teacher.

T'ai chi

Often called 'meditation in motion', t'ai chi consists of an interlinked series of slow, flowing movements that have been shown to relax the muscles and nervous system. T'ai chi is suitable for all ages, but it is a particularly good form of exercise for old people. Of the five types of t'ai chi, yang is the Western world's favourite. It is a series of postures that link to form one long flow. Its short form has 24 movements and takes 5-10 minutes. The longer form has 108 movements and takes up to 40 minutes to complete. An instructor will stress the importance of performing the flexing and extended moves with a relaxed sense of continuity, precision and a natural flow of breath.

Qi gong

This martial art was first practised in 200 BC by Chinese doctors. 'Qi' means energy and 'gong' means practice. But some claim its proper title is 'the curing of illness through muscle movement'. The exercises – which stress the importance of posture and, like t'ai chi, are performed in a slow, relaxed way – stimulate the body's source of qi.

Wing chun

A popular form of kung fu, wing chun is an ideal martial art for women. It teaches a method of using the least

amount of energy for self-defence and keeping a good position in which you can attack an enemy's weaker areas or acupressure points. It relies more on technique than force, more on sensitivity than strength.

Capoeira

Capoeira is a non-contact fighting dance that hails from Brazil. The aim is not to win but to outwit your opponent by using swift, low movements – flips, cartwheels and handstands. Good for toning the bottom and thigh area, with regular practice it increases cardiovascular fitness and improves flexibility.

Kalari

A form of self-defence, kalari was first practised by (male and female) sword-wielding warriors in Kerala, southern India. Weapons such as swords and sticks are used but only at advanced levels. Like asthanga yoga, kalari begins and ends with salutations. Gentle movements work gradually to an intense physical workout. Through each session, participants are urged to focus on their vital source – the unification of breath and movement.

Judo

This sport offers a better method of self-defence training than any other sport. A centuries-old method of Japanese unarmed combat, judo was taken up as a modern physical activity

in 1882 when a Japanese professor established it as the country's form of physical education. Soon it was adopted as a way of apprehending law breakers by Japan's police force (it still is today). Judo training can start at any age and participants across the world range in age from eight to eighty-five.

Karate

Translated into English, 'karate' means 'the way of the empty hand'. Dating back to the Ming Dynasty (1368-1644), this form of self-defence – which uses no weapons but the body – was derived from the disciplines of Buddhism on the Japanese island of Okinawa.

Kendo

Kendo is the way of the sword, the Japanese martial art of fencing which reaches back thousands of years to the sword-wielding warriors known as the Bushido or the Samurai. Bamboo shinal are used to strike the opponent. A match is usually the best of three strikes. Those practising Kendo today range from children to retirees.

Climbing

Free your mind and strengthen your body. Climbing requires concentration and footwork skill. But it rewards participants with a positive mental focus and a total endurance boost.

Rock climbing

Rock climbing demands a certain amount of agility and fitness but most instructors claim that beginners can attempt basic grades and master how to use the equipment – rock boots (which are made of hard rubber) and ropes (which must be kept tight to prohibit falling) – as well as the knot-tying skills they require (figure-of-eights, clove hitches). Bouldering, a technique of climbing which is done without ropes on high, free-standing rocks varying in height from 3 to 15 m (10 to 50 ft), is best left to advanced climbers. Instruction is essential to show novices technique and even at advanced stages, an instructor can point out mistakes and show you how to improve your ability.

Indoor climbing

This is a fast-growing sport. According to the British Mountaineering Council, there are now 150,000 climbers in the UK. The ratio of male to female climbers is eight to two. Manmade climbing walls – built of resin to resemble real cliffs, though indoor walls are equipped with handholds and footholds – were first used to offer rock climbers a weatherproofed training outlet. But today, new climbers view it as a method of keeping fit; 15 per cent of indoor climbers have never experienced the sensation of reaching a real peak.

Tree climbing

This form of climbing also requires ropes and knot-tying skills. Adults in the US are taking part in treetop climbing for several different reasons: to relive childhood memories or to get closer to nature.

Water power

The great thing about swimming and other pool-based exercises is that they offer total relaxation in tandem with a vigorous workout.

Swimming

If you feel self-conscious in a swimming costume, remember one thing – bikini diets don't work. But swimming three times a week for 25 to 45 minutes per session is as much of a body conditioner as an aerobics class. Swimming is the best form of overall exercise according to personal instructor Steven Shaw. Shaw, who is trained in the Alexander technique, is the co-author of *The Shaw Method* which brings thinking on swimming up-to-date. He believes that swimming performed correctly greatly benefits breathing and alignment and improves psychological outlook. In the pool, Shaw does not encourage the use of float boards or other equipment. A great top-to-toe toning workout, he claims, comes when a swimmer is concentrating on the technique of each stroke as well as varying strokes during a swim. He also promotes power swimming – interval training which alternates fast lengths with slow during a swim. Sprinting every five laps during a fifty lap swim should burn fat and build stamina.

Relaxing, warming up, cooling down and proper breathing will maximize the effectiveness of a workout in the pool. Stretching pool-side is not necessary but it will make you feel more limber. A few slow lengths at the start and finish of a swim should suffice. When it comes to breathing, try not to take in gulps of air. Breathe gently and evenly as you normally would, and never hold your breath. Some experts say that when your head goes back in the water once you've inhaled (to the left or right of your shoulder), it should look straight ahead instead of straight down. This allows the windpipe to open, so you can exhale easier.

Remember, coaches are not just for children's swim classes. Having a pool-side personal trainer – to monitor your strokes and heart rate – could maximize the effectiveness of an aquatic workout.

Aqua aerobics

If you can't swim, don't be put off by exercise in a pool. Aqua aerobics offers a safe and effective workout. Eighty per cent of impact stress on the joints and bones is absorbed by the water. Furthermore, water offers the body 12 times more resistance to work against than the air (the Chinese have long recognized the power this resistance offers for increasing strength and recuperation). The resistance is low-impact and rather than it moving in one direction, it is multi-directional so opposing muscle groups work at the same time. The movements performed also create drag and turbulence with the result that once speed is increased, the resistance does too, so the muscles work harder.

You may find aqua aerobics easier than a gym-based fitness class. Because of water's buoyancy, pool-based exercise programmes are popular with less co-ordinated people. Water helps circulation and some claim its massaging effect helps to reduce cellulite.

How to monitor your heart rate

Working as hard and as long as you can is the most efficient way to use up calories and reduce body fat. To measure how hard you are working, you should know what your target heart rate zone is and plan to exercise in that zone to get the best results from your workout.

During exercise, your heart rate goes up. The harder you work, the faster your heart beats. Everyone has a maximum heart rate, the fastest it can possibly beat. Calculating how close your heart rate is to its maximum during exercise enables you to check the intensity of your workout. However, you should never work at maximum intensity.

To find your maximum heart rate zone, subtract your age from 220. If you are 30, your maximum heart rate is 190. To monitor your heart rate, find your pulse point, count how many times you feel a beat over six seconds and then multiply that total by ten. It is easy to miss beats, so investing in an electronic heart rate monitor might be worth considering. Some gyms rent them out.

wellbeing and the way you look

Part of being human means judging and being judged by appearances. When we meet someone for the first time, all our senses are alert, picking up on small details to build the bigger picture. Height, age, hair colour, size and clothes are perceived in an instant, but then a sense of the individual's confidence, sensitivity, vitality and outlook on life emerges and that is where the fascination lies. Communication, character, individuality – these all leave a deeper impression.

Our own self-image is bound up in our society's ideal. Reinforced through films and magazines, we assume a collective awe towards this young, slim, smooth-skinned, glossy haired creature, but to most of us it is a version that has nothing whatever to do with real life. Nursing comparisons usually fuels negative feelings, which can batter the self-esteem. Of course appearances matter, but only in so far as how much they matter to you. Body care is as much about lifestyle as it is about cosmetic applications. After all, there is only so much a product can do to conceal a junk food diet, a nicotine habit, late nights and a hangover.

The sound, common sense philosophy to looking good runs along the lines of: don't drink excessive amounts of alcohol, don't smoke, keep your skin and hair clean, take regular exercise, get plenty of sleep, eat a well-balanced diet and master your relaxation techniques. This approach gives you the best possible chance of remaining fit, looking great and feeling happy for life. End of story.

Or is it? How is this great ideal of looking good and feeling better going to be achieved? First, be realistic. Look at what you want to change in your life and make small adjustments to the routines you already have, adapting them around your

self-worth

It is important to do what it takes to make you feel good about yourself – not slavishly following the latest fads which will leave you worn out and (financially) worse off.

condition

Look after your skin, hair, nails and teeth to keep them in good condition for the whole of your life. Value your body and enjoy it.

routines

We all have unique body care routines, which evolve to suit our needs and fit in with our lifestyles. They should be viewed as a healthy part of everyday life, developed to help make you feel self-assured and comfortable with your body.

nurture

Make your self-care rituals an expression of self-worth, savour the moments, relish the results and nurture your wellbeing.

realism

Heredity also plays an important part in the way you look – think what your family tendency is and make a realistic decision about how much you can change. You can then live with the problem, conceal it or treat it.

established lifestyle. Don't attempt to go for the drastic, all at once life-altering solutions, because failing to meet your (unreasonable) expectations is bound to leave you disappointed and despondent. These are not the feelings to enhance a positive love of self, so take it easy. And think positive. The unconscious mind follows the strongest thought, so say to yourself what you want to hear and that will immediately help boost your self-esteem.

Back to basics

The fundamental aim is to keep your skin and hair clean and in good condition.

To do this you need to protect them from repeated environmental assault – sun, wind, pollution, central heating, salt or chlorinated water can all have a damaging effect. Body care routines need to adapt with the seasons, your age and with different activities. As far as products are concerned, simply use what is safe, feels good and does not make unrealistic claims. There are many straightforward, time-honoured ways to cleanse and protect the skin and hair with products available to blend a traditional holistic approach with state-of-the-art technology.

What's age got to do with it?

Age will eventually and inevitably slow you down. It will alter your body but – barring disease – not your mind.

Dreading the passage of time only creates misery and stress which may bring with it far more ill-effects than the ageing process itself. 'Age prints more wrinkles on the mind than it does on the face', wrote the French essayist Montaigne four centuries ago. In other words, it is an attitude thing. A rational, philosophical approach to the passing years, reflecting on what you've learnt and achieved beats lunging for the latest anti-wrinkle formula. We should try and enjoy our bodies at every age. There are youthful looks – and then there is everything else. Life offers too many other fascinations to dwell on a wrinkle, so try to cultivate healthier habits and invest your time and energy in positive pastimes.

The (not so simple) route to good-looking skin

Drink eight to ten glasses of water every day. Water helps to flush out your system and eliminate toxins.

Exercise regularly. Just 30 minutes of exercise every day – maybe a brisk walk or a cycle ride – brings blood and nutrients to the skin and tones the muscles.

Get plenty of sleep. It will not only make you feel better, you'll look better too.

Always wear a sunscreen when outdoors. Particularly on pale skin, the sun accounts for nearly all the signs that are associated with ageing.

Eat plenty of raw fruit and vegetables, preferably organic.

Moisturize your skin from the outside with hydrating ingredients.

Seal in the moisture with naturally based vegetable oils.

Gently exfoliate your skin to lift away dead skin cells and stimulate cell renewal.

Cut out smoking. Smoking destroys the vitamin C that keeps your collagen fibres attached to your skin and your skin attached to the fatty pads beneath them.

Learn how to relax, unwind and eliminate stress.

Skin care

Skin is the body's largest living organ, weighing between 1.8 and 2.7 kg (4 and 6 lb). It provides a protective barrier against harmful bacteria, prevents water loss and helps bodies maintain a constant core temperature. The billions of nerve endings and fibres in the skin transmit information about the external environment back to the brain. Emotions such as anger and embarrassment make skin flush and we may sweat in response to fear, or pale with shock. The skin and psyche are so closely linked that emotional problems and stress can trigger eczema or spots, likewise acne can have a deep psychological effect on – particularly teenage – self-esteem.

Because the colour and characteristics of your skin are determined by genetic inheritance, it is as individual as you are. No one skin care regime is suitable for all people, so tailor your routines to reflect your skin type and lifestyle – and be alert to the changes that come about with age. At around twenty-five, the skin's oil production begins to slow and hormonal shifts throughout life alter skin, so adjust your approach accordingly. Cleaning your skin thoroughly and regularly is the most important starting point of any skin care regime.

Cleansing the face

Michel Tournier has said that, 'There is only one sure way of knowing whether you love somebody, it is when their face inspires more physical desire than any other part of their body.'

If you cleanse properly you will get rid of dead skin cells and toxins, remove all make-up, dirt, air-borne grime and chemical pollutants, clear out clogged pores, and eliminate infection causing bacteria – and all this without stripping away the skin's natural oils.

Follow a basic routine: cleanse, freshen and moisturize in the morning and cleanse, exfoliate and moisturize at night. If you use the right products, you will be doing just about all the good you can for your skin – on the outside.

Soaps not designed specifically for the face can be too harsh and drying. It is better to use a cleansing face bar, cleansing face wash, cleansing milk, lotion or a cream.

Follow with a mild freshening toner to remove all traces of dirt and cleanser and always finish with a moisturizer. Avoid very abrasive scrubs on your face altogether. Use warm – not cold – water when you wash your face as it will help to dissolve oil and dirt. If the water is very hot, it can lead to tiny broken veins. If you feel like a bit of do-it-yourself, try the honey treatment outlined below.

Spotty skin needs special care, but that doesn't mean more washing or using harsh chemicals. Wash twice a day with a cleansing soap-free face wash or bar to remove excess oil, clear the pores and control the spread of bacteria. Tone with witch hazel mixed with some water or a saline solution and use a light, probably oil-free moisturizer that doesn't block the pores. Only use a very gentle exfoliating lotion or else you may stimulate the sebaceous glands to produce more oil. Face masks are very useful to improve the condition of spotty skin. Either buy a suitable one or make your own turmeric and honey face mask and apply it directly to spotty areas (see page 142).

Wash before exercise

If you take off your make-up before you exercise, your skin is clean and sweating acts as an extra-cleanse. If it is clogged with make-up it won't be able to cleanse itself so efficiently. When you sweat don't wipe your face with your hands but use a clean towel.

Cleansing honey

Honey is a good moisturizer and suitable for all skin types. Runny honey is the easiest to use. Look out for manuka honey, which is made with nectar from the tea tree and is particularly soothing. Rub the honey onto your face with smooth circular movements, then dip your fingers in hot water and repeat. The warmth from the water encourages the skin to soften and helps shift embedded dirt and dead skin cells. Massage for a few minutes then rinse off with warm water and pat your face dry.

Ayurvedic skin care

Ayurveda means life and knowledge. It has developed from 6,000 years of Eastern wisdom relating to health and body care. The basic tenet states: if you can't eat it, don't rub it on your skin. This may sound like a treatment for the purists but natural skin care remedies are highly suitable for people with sensitive skin. Olive, sunflower, coconut, sesame and avocado oils, honey and oatmeal – they are probably all in your kitchen and it takes just a small leap of imagination to think of them as your body care products.

Skin care in the kitchen

Olive oil: used in skin care for thousands of years, it is also suitable for conditioning dry hair.

Coconut oil: it has good natural cleansing properties as well as being a moisturizer and hair conditioner.

Sunflower oil: excellent basic oil for massage blends and body lotions.

Avocado oil: the flesh contains nearly 50 per cent oil. It is one of the best natural oils for soothing very dry skin. Pulp it up and put it on.

Cider vinegar: useful for restoring the pH balance to the skin and for adding to the final rinsing water after washing your hair.

Honey: a soothing moisturizer.

Oatmeal: excellent for treating over-dry, irritated or sensitive skin. Porridge oat flakes added to a warm bath soften the water and moisturize the skin. (Tie them inside a muslin cloth if you don't want to sit in them.)

Using natural oils

All skins: sweet almond oil and jojoba oils are excellent cleansers, regardless of skin type. Massage gently into your face and remove with a warm damp cloth.

Dry or mature skin: wheatgerm oil is very rich and can help improve the condition of dry skin. Add it to your night-time moisturizer to give your skin a super-rich moisturizing dose. Carrot oil is an excellent moisturizer used by itself, or use it to boost another moisture cream. Add it to oatmeal for an effective scrub.

Skin protection

Twentieth-century medicine has almost doubled our expected lifespan, but advances in the science of ageing march on. Science has discovered that the rate of ageing is controlled by how quickly the tips of the chromosomes break down. These tips, called telomers, act like biological clocks. Every time the cell divides, the hands of the telomer clock advance and the cell gets one step closer to death. Drugs are now being developed that might some day prevent the breakdown of telomers and essentially stop the ageing process forever.

Until that time, if you want your skin to carry you through for a respectable 70 or 80 years, it needs protection – particularly from the sun. The first sunscreens were developed in the 16th century from thin glazes of egg-white. This was at a time when white skin was so admired in England that women wore masks held on by buttons clamped between their teeth. A tan only became fashionable in the 20th century between the wars when Coco Chanel started the misguided trend for nut brown skin. Several decades and millions of skin cancers later, we understand how damaging ultraviolet rays can be.

Many people accept skin changes such as wrinkles and blotches as an inevitable part of ageing. In fact, they are caused by over-exposure to the sun. Take a look at the skin on your inner arm where the sun doesn't usually reach and you will probably see a marked difference between that area and the back of your hands.

There is now enough compelling evidence to believe that over-exposure to the sun is the single biggest factor in the development of skin cancer. In the UK, as many as 40,000 people a year are diagnosed with one form or another. The most dangerous, malignant melanomas are thought to be related to short, sharp overdoses of sun, just the sort of exposure people in the UK often get on an intense two-week holiday abroad. It is essential to enjoy an active outdoor life, but always protect yourself from the sun's radiation. For the best protection, keep legs, arms and the back of the neck covered with clothes made of a tightly woven fabric. Wear a wide-brimmed hat and wrap-around sunglasses.

Summer skin

A tan was once strongly associated with wellbeing. Now a greater understanding of its dangers has led to a shift in thinking, which means we no longer equate health, happiness and success with a deep tan.

Use a protective sunscreen all year round but make it a higher SPF in the summer. Apply it half an hour before going into the sun and at least after every 40 minutes if using water-resistant, or 80 minutes if using water-proof products, when you are outside, and always after swimming or towel drying.

Never allow your skin to burn. The damage is permanent and years later it may manifest itself as a skin cancer.

Shelter babies and young children from direct rays. They have especially tender skin so keep young infants covered up in the shade with plenty of sunscreen and sun products containing high SPFs. Remember that ultraviolet rays can be reflected off the sand and water.

Don't overdo it. Peak radiation hours are between 10 am and 4 pm, so try and avoid direct exposure between these hours.

If you are serious about protecting your skin, you should wear a sunscreen while outdoors all year round, even on cloudy days. When choosing a sunscreen, the simple rule is: the higher the sun protection factor number, the more protection it offers. The number relates to the amount of times longer you can stay in the sun without getting burnt as opposed to wearing no sunscreen. Dermatologists usually recommend a minimum sunscreen of SPF 15 which means your skin will be protected an average 15 times longer with the sunscreen than without it. Choose a sunscreen that screens out UVA and UVB rays: UVB primarily causes sunburn, wrinkles, dark spots and skin cancer; UVA is primarily responsible for premature ageing and increases the long-term effects of sunburn. It can also penetrate glass, so the skin is vulnerable near windows and in cars. Together UVA and UVB form an aggressive and intrusive combination.

Moisture is a must

Sebum is the skin's built-in moisturizer. All skin has it but those with too much tend to oily skin and in extreme cases, acne. People with dry skin may not generate enough sebum. Moisturizing your skin is a delicate balance between adding water and preventing evaporation. Its function is to maintain soft skin by creating a watertight seal to keep up the water level in the outermost layer and preventing continuous evaporation from the surface. Moisturizers have many added skin benefits. Some contain sunscreens and herbal extracts to help calm skin irritations, others have soothing ingredients and help shield the skin from polluted city streets. Some of the most effective moisturizers are pure nut and seed oils. Rub sweet almond oil into dry skin before bathing and emerge with soft, supple skin and no need to further moisturize.

Winter skin

Prepare and protect your skin well for the extreme changes in temperature and the added drying effects of central heating.

Because the upper area of the cheeks below the eyes have the fewest oil glands, it is where winter dryness shows first. Use a heavier moisturizer even if your skin is acne-prone (in which case use a water-based rather than oil-based cream.)

Protect your face by pulling your collar up, hat down and wrapping a scarf over as much of your face as possible. It will help prevent the little red broken capillaries.

Lips only have a thin layer of skin cells compared to elsewhere on the body, so you need a good barrier cream to keep them soft and supple through the winter.

Lips lose moisture rapidly and licking them leaves them more dehydrated, flaky and prone to chapping.

Exfoliate and moisturize as you do the rest of your face and always keep a waxy salve to hand to protect against the elements.

Intensive winter skin moisturizer

This rich moisturizing face mask with a gentle exfoliating action is also a useful treatment for dry or mature hands.

1 tbsp plain live yoghurt
1 egg yolk
½ tsp honey
1 tsp mayonnaise

Mix all the ingredients to a smooth paste and apply to clean, dry skin. Leave on for 15-20 minutes, then rinse with warm water and pat your face dry.

Revitalizing treatments

Exfoliation

Once you incorporate exfoliation into your routine, you will probably never stop. It leaves your skin feeling smooth and looking fine. Exfoliation lifts off the top layer of dead skin cells, dirt and sebum to reveal a new layer of skin cells beneath. This stimulates the blood circulation which helps rid the area of waste products. As the skin ages, the production of new cells slows down, but exfoliation can accelerate cell renewal and help smooth the surface layer.

Exfoliation can be chemical or mechanical. Chemical exfoliants include alpha-hydroxy acids (AHAs or fruit acids) derived from sour milk, apples, lemons, sugar cane or wine. Mechanical exfoliation means using scrubs and abrasive cloths such as flannels and loofahs.

AHAs are incorporated into lotions which gradually peel off the outer layers of skin and accelerate the production of new cells. They can make the skin look smoother and brighter, but they can also cause an adverse reaction, a rash or irritation. If this happens, stop using the product immediately. AHAs have hogged the cosmetic limelight, but beta-hydroxy acids such as salicylic acid are said to penetrate deeper into oil-clogged pores and be less likely to irritate the skin.

If you use exfoliants, be very careful to apply the right grades of scrub to the appropriate area. For example, scrubs are available for heels and as an all-over body boost – but for the face, stick to products that are specially formulated for this area so that dead skin cells will be gently sloughed off. Generally avoid delicate areas such as under the eyes.

Steam clean

To get the best from a facial scrub, try a once-a-week herbal steam first. Add a few drops of lavender essential oil to a big bowl of hot (not boiling) water or infuse some fresh herb mixtures (dried herbs will do). For normal skin use lavender; for dry skin, camomile; for oily or combination skins, mint and lemon peel are a successful combination. Cover your head with a towel and make a tent of it as you lean over the bowl, trapping the steam. Enjoy the feeling for about 5 minutes, then pat dry and apply your chosen scrub.

Exfoliating skin mask

1 tbsp finely ground oatmeal
1 tbsp plain live yoghurt
1/2 apple, freshly grated
2 tsp fresh lemon juice

This mask is full of the natural AHAs found in commercial skin creams which act as a gentle exfoliant and remove build-up of sebum. Oatmeal has a soothing effect on irritated, blotchy skin. Mix the oatmeal and yoghurt to a paste then add the apple and lemon juice and stir well. Apply to clean dry skin and relax for 15-20 minutes before rinsing off with warm water and patting the skin dry.

The simplest exfoliator

Use one ripe papaya. The enzyme called papain in papaya literally dissolves keratin, the hardened protein found in the dead skin cells on your skin. Slice off large pieces of the papaya skin, remove the seeds, and then rub the fleshy inside part over your freshly cleansed face and neck for a couple of minutes. Rinse thoroughly with cool water and pat dry.

Other face relaxing techniques

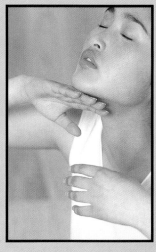

The Bharti Vyas lion pose

Fingertip tapping
This is another quick way to relax tense facial muscles. Drum the balls of your fingers around your eyes, forehead, cheeks, mouth and even over your scalp.

This is an exercise to firm up the face and neck muscles. Breathe in, then open your mouth as wide as it will go, stick out your tongue as far as possible and breathe out slowly, while looking at the ceiling without raising your head or straining your eyes.

Chin slap
Stick your chin out and use the backs of both hands to alternately beat out a stimulating massage – firm but not hard.

Sleep

Sleep is the cornerstone of health and wellbeing. In sleep, the body releases human growth hormone which revitalizes the body and restores energy. A good sleep should leave you with a sense of vitality that lasts all day. One way to sleep better is to develop a regular sleeping pattern. Another is to eat certain foods which contain the amino acid tryptophan. This chemical triggers sleep, so eat some tryptophan-rich pumpkin seeds before bed and you may fall asleep more quickly and sleep more soundly.

The acupressure face-lift

This face-lift procedure is based on techniques from Chinese acupuncture, Japanese shiatsu and Western neuromuscular massage. It is a quick, effective, non-invasive and completely free face-lift.

Acupressure is based on the same system of points and meridians as acupuncture but with acupressure you simply use the fingertips to stimulate specific points on the body instead of inserting needles. Massaging these acupoints creates warmth that converts into a minute electrical charge which stimulates the muscles, nerves and lymphatic system, clearing the energy pathways known as meridians. The meridians run from head to toe and each one corresponds with certain vital organs.

Acupoints are cup-shaped. You can feel them as slight depressions just below the surface of the skin. If the points are blocked or congested, the flow of energy throughout the body is imbalanced. When the point is pressed it helps restore the body's natural impulse towards balance.

Devotees of the acupressure face-lift say it doesn't just revitalize tired tissue on your face, but can also have far-reaching effects on the rest of your body and wellbeing. You may find your headaches disappear, your digestion improves, your ability to handle stress is enhanced and your skin tone is improved.

◎ Each point is stimulated for less than 1 minute so the lift takes 20 minutes.

◎ Once you know how to do it, you can do it any time, anywhere and noticeable results can be achieved rapidly.

◎ Use your middle finger or your index finger with the pad of your middle finger on top. Whenever you complete each area or whenever you feel any muscles need a rest, shake out your hands and relax.

◎ Press firmly but not aggressively and use very small circular movements, never drag the skin.

◎ Whether you are massaging, cleansing or applying make-up on the upper eye area always circle from the inner corner out, and on the lower eye area from the outer corner in.

Acupoints

Point 1
At the hairline, directly above the eyes. Circle inwards.

Point 2
Just below Point 1. Midway between your hairline and eyebrows. Circle inwards.

Point 3
At the inside of your eye sockets at the base of the bridge of your nose. Lodge the thumbs in the corner then rotate them up and push up onto the bone under the eyebrows. Do not touch the eyes.

Point 4
At the far end of the eyebrows. Circle outwards.

Point 5
Outside corner of the eyes. Circle outwards.

Point 6
On the lower ridge of the eye socket, in line with the centre of the eye, a slight depression on the top of the cheekbone. Circle outwards.

Point 7
Just below 6: a depression in your cheek, on a line with the flare of your nostrils. Circle outwards.

Point 8
Midway between the bottom of your nose and the top of your lip. Firm clockwise circles.

Point 9
Midway between lower lip and chin. Small clockwise circles.

Point 10
On the muscle at the jaw hinge. Find the depression with mouth slightly open. Circle to the back of your head.

Eye care

The skin around the eyes is very thin and sensitive with very few oil glands. Fine lines, puffiness, dark circles and a loss of elasticity are the most common signs of sun damage, a dissipated lifestyle and age.

However, heredity also plays an important part so before you embark on a programme, think what your family tendency is and realistically decide whether you can change it. You can then live with the problems, conceal them or treat them. The latter course of action means eating better, sleeping more and applying a light moisturizer to the area. Use fragrance-free creams to help prevent irritation to the eye area. Key natural ingredients to look for include eyebright (a soothing herb), aloe vera and allantoin.

Use a sunscreen when outdoors all year round and wear wrap-around sunglasses in the sun. Avoid smoking (the eyes naturally squint to avoid the smoke, creating fine lines) and rubbing below the eyes. When you are applying a cream, do it gently to avoid dragging, and circle from the outside corner to the inside corner on the under eye area.

Some dedicated beauty therapists advise sleeping on your back as gravity works to pull the skin backwards. If you sleep on the same side night after night, you simply press the same wrinkles into your face. The jury's still out on this one.

Hand care

We use our hands for greeting and to touch each other in comfort, communication and healing. They are an expressive tool, emphasizing our most passionately held feelings.

It is essential to keep them clean. Infections are frequently spread, particularly among children, by touching hands and then rubbing eyes so it would be better for us all to cough and sneeze into the crook of the arm rather than into our hands. How often we wash our hands depends on what we've been doing, but almost any contact with others will expose us to infection, though some exposure is essential to build up our natural defences with antibodies. If you have children in the house who tend to regard hand-washing as a chore and are not very thorough, use an antibacterial hand wash to help them get really clean. Keep nails clean by using a scrubbing brush under your nails every day.

Always wear gloves outside in winter. Use a moisturizing hand wash and, if possible, rub in a moisturizer after washing. Hands are generally immersed in water more often than the rest of the body and they are nearly always exposed to the elements. For both these reasons they need more help to maintain moisture levels so carry a small bottle of intensive hand cream with you – one with an SPF will help avoid brown 'age' spots. Wear rubber gloves for chores and here's a tip for startling results – moisturize your hands before bed (wheatgerm oil or sunflower oil is ideal) and slip them into cotton gloves (or socks) overnight. You really will wake up to smoother, softer hands.

A personal manicure

Exfoliate your hands by mixing a few drops of almond oil with some salt and rubbing it gently over hands and nails. Rinse off and your hands will feel wonderfully smooth. Use sharp nail clippers to cut your nails, working from one side to the other – don't just lop off the tip as this will damage the nail. Use an emery board to shape your nails and file from side to centre in one smooth stroke. Metal nail files can be damaging. Soften cuticles with a rich moisturizer or almond oil, and push them back gently with an orange stick covered in cotton wool. Bare nails in good condition look great – you can make them shine with a few strokes from a nail buffer.

Quick fix for long-term nail health

Encourage strong, healthy growth by stimulating the flow of blood to the nail bed, ensuring improved delivery of oxygen and essential nutrients. Bend the fingers of both hands in towards your palms, and place the two sets of nails together. With relaxed hands, rub them against each other for a minute. With practice, you can tuck your thumbs under and get them into the routine too.

Moisturizing hand massage

Every time you moisturize your hands, give them a mini-massage. Use small circular movements over your knuckles and finger joints and follow by a pulling motion to ease the joints. Use your thumbs to massage the backs of your hands, smoothing up towards the wrists. Include the acupressure point on your hand where your thumb and forefinger are joined – this point is related to the large intestine and to the flow of energy to the face.

Foot relief

A cold footbath is a wonderful way to revive tired feet. Alternating between warm and cold baths will boost the circulation and may help prevent varicose veins in the legs. Add a few drops of lemon or peppermint essential oil to leave the feet smelling fresh. Moisturize and massage with peppermint-based oils and lotions, particularly after a warm bath.

Wearing high heels will throw you off-balance, disrupt your posture and can cause back ache. Your ankles, heels and toes can also suffer – but then if you wear high heels you know that already. To prevent the just-bought-them, can't-wear-them mistake, buy shoes in the afternoon so they fit when your feet are slightly swollen; and if you are a slave to the heel, vary their height from day to day.

On a regular basis – perhaps once a week – use a pumice stone to exfoliate hard skin and moisturize as often as you can. The ideal time for all-over moisturizing is after a bath or shower, while your skin is still damp, as it 'locks in' the moisture. As with hands, if you apply a rich, intensive moisturizing cream or natural oil to your feet before bed and slip them into cotton socks overnight, you'll wake up to smoother, softer feet than you thought possible.

A soothing foot balm

1 tsp malt vinegar
1 tub plain yoghurt

Stir the malt vinegar into the yoghurt and rub over the feet and between the toes. Leave on for 5 minutes and rinse off with lukewarm water.

A personal pedicure

Rub a rich moisturizer or a little pure almond oil around the toenails after your bath or shower to keep the cuticles soft and well-conditioned. Wrap cotton wool around an orange stick (or use a cotton bud) to very gently push the cuticles back and make your feet look well cared for. In-growing toenails can result from tights and shoes worn too small and incorrect nail cutting. Use scissors and cut them straight across taking care not to cut them too short. Sharp corners can be carefully smoothed with a coarse emery board (not a metal file).

Common problems

Athlete's foot is an infectious fungus which thrives in warm, moist places and spreads without direct contact, so avoid sharing towels. Apply tea tree oil between the toes to treat and prevent athlete's foot. Cotton wool soaked in vinegar and lemon wedges rubbed between the toes make effective natural treatments.

A verruca is a wart caused by a virus which is also picked up in moist, sweaty conditions. Sixty per cent of verrucas go on their own within two years – but if that seems like a long time and the verruca is painful, use an over-the-counter wart removal formula or see a state-registered chiropodist.

Bath therapy

Perhaps there is some long-buried atavistic sense linking a wallow in a warm bath to the time we flopped around in the primeval mud. Whatever, it feels good.

Hippocrates, the 'father of medicine', said the way to health was a scented bath and a massage every day. Bathing is certainly one of the simplest, cheapest and most therapeutic treatments available. Twenty minutes in a bath sprinkled with a natural oil such as evening primrose oil, or fragrant essential oils will not only soothe and moisturize your skin, it will also help to relax or revitalize your mind (depending on which oils you use). Your mind plays a big part in skin care. The root of many skin care problems – especially rashes, eczema and acne – is often stress.

Aromatherapy

Single essential oils form the basis of aromatherapy. It is their effect on mood and mind that give them their special fascination. They are highly concentrated so are usually diluted in carrier oils for treatment, with the rare exception of lavender and tea tree. If you use full strength oils be very careful to read directions for dosage when adding them to your bath. For more information see pages 180-5.

A bath for a boost

A cool bath is a fantastic pick-me-up, hard to take but well worth it for the surge of energy you feel afterwards, but remember that this experience is only for people in good health (they can be too much of a shock to the system). Try one in the morning to wake up you and your muscles, or at the end of the day to revitalize you before going out; it's particularly energizing to have a cold plunge after a hot shower. Alternatively, you could add a few drops of reviving essential oil to a warm bath if you felt like a less challenging boost. Refreshing oils include geranium, rosemary, peppermint and lemon.

Relaxing bathing

To make the most of bath time, prepare your bath well, following these simple guidelines.

The water should be pleasantly warm. Too hot and it may over-stimulate your system, dehydrate the skin and damage delicate capillaries (leading to red spider veins).

Add a few drops of an essential oil. For example, lavender essential oil is reputed to ease aches and pains and soothe the nervous system. Sandalwood essential oil is reported to calm, aid relaxation and induce sleep. It is particularly suitable for dry skin.

Deep breathing is a wonderful way to induce relaxation. Inhale deeply through your nose for a count of four, hold for eight counts, exhale slowly through your mouth for a count of twelve. Repeat five times.

Now lie back and close your eyes. Relax all your muscles from the tips of your fingers to the tips of your toes thinking down from your facial muscles through your neck to your spine, arms and legs.

Music can distract a racing mind, eliminate extraneous sounds and relieve stress.

Candlelight is easier on the eye than electric bulbs.

Shut the bathroom door to keep fragrant vapours in and distractions out.

Hair play

Hair and nails are made of the same basic material – keratin – and whatever you consume to benefit one will also benefit the other.

Like skin, the hair is lubricated by the body's own protective oil called sebum and it is overactive sebaceous glands on the scalp that cause greasy hair. If your hair looks good, then you are probably treating your hair, scalp and body right, so there is clearly no need to change a thing. The hair root cells on the head are the most rapidly developing in the body and are extremely sensitive to changes in diet, hormones, stress levels and even weather. When the outer casing of the hair, called the cuticle, lies flat, the hair reflects light and looks shiny and healthy. If the cuticles are roughed up by excess heat, harsh chemicals, salt water or too much sun, the hair looks dull and dry. Washing your hair in excessively hot water will also exacerbate a dry scalp and can have a dehydrating effect.

There are four basic conditions which can affect the scalp – dryness, oiliness, flakiness and dandruff. You could have one or a combination of these. Seek advice from a professional who is familiar with naturally based ingredients rather than harsh chemicals which may have contributed to the problem in the first place. Poor circulation in the scalp is the underlying cause of many hair problems so a scalp massage will relieve tension and stimulate the blood supply (see page 139). Second to washing and conditioning your hair, this is one of the most beneficial things you can possibly do to it.

Conditioning hair

The power of a healthy-looking, shiny head of hair to make you feel good cannot be over-estimated. Like the rest of your body, your hair is affected by diet, exercise and stress. Unlike the rest of your body you can change its colour, shape and style on a whim depending on whether you feel flamboyant or conservative.

To work your hair around your mood you need to keep it in good condition. Wash as often as you need, probably twice a week. If it looks good, don't change a thing. If it doesn't, try altering your shampoo, your conditioner and the frequency with which you wash it. Always rinse for twice as long as you think necessary (with clean water not bath water floating with scum). Cut down on heated appliances and keep your hair covered while in the sun.

For hair to be soft and easy to style it needs to be well cared for. Conditioners and treatments protect the outer layer of the hair from damage by heated styling. The sauna is the ideal place to treat your hair to a deep-conditioning treatment as heat helps intensify the effect. Apply it before you get into the sauna and then leave it on for 20 minutes.

For really shiny, vibrant hair, treat it to a weekly deep-conditioning treatment or hair mask. You can combine this with a head massage using coconut oil, an effective way to stimulate your scalp and the hair follicles. In Asian culture, thick, lustrous hair is often maintained with scalp massage. Poor circulation in the scalp can be the cause of many hair problems but in addition to benefiting your hair, scalp massage will release tension, clear your head and lighten your mood. This is why so many hairdressers now practise it. Even if the haircut is unspeakably bad, you won't care so much or complain so loudly after a good head massage.

Simple solutions for problem hair

For dry hair, separate an egg, beat the yolk and white separately, then fold together and massage into hair. Leave for 5 minutes. Rinse with warm water.

For dandruff, beat 2 egg yolks into 115ml (¼ pint) warm water. Massage into the scalp, leave for 10 minutes, then rinse. Rinse again with 2 tsps of vinegar in 225ml (½ pint) cool water.

For flat hair, dilute 1 cup of flat beer with 3 cups of water and wash hair. Rinse thoroughly.

To add body, make a paste with mashed bananas. Apply it to damp hair, leave for 15 minutes, then shampoo out.

Massaging your own head

The thin layer of muscle which covers the skull tightens as tension arises, causing headaches and restricting blood supply to the hair follicles, affecting the hair's condition. Self-massage is easy, especially when you are washing your hair.

Stroke your head lightly all over from the forehead to the back of the neck and from the temples, over the ears to the neck.

Make small firm circles over the scalp, working from front to back with thumb and fingertips – particularly where tension builds around the ears and base of the skull. Manipulate the scalp and help loosen it.

Stroke all over your hair gently, and then grab a handful at the roots and pull quite firmly.

Release the hair and glide your fingers through it. Alternate the hands rhythmically pulling with one and gliding with the other to pull out the tension.

Position your hands on either side of your head – fingers over the ears, heels of your hands by the temples. Press your hands in gently for a few seconds. Release pressure slowly and glide hands up the side of your head and off the top. Repeat several times.

Coconut oil is perfect for head massage. It leaves a protective coating on the hair after washing which holds in moisture and provides a barrier against the sun and heated hair appliances. Olive and almond oil are both possible substitutes.

Mouth matters

Smiling and laughing is an uplifting therapy and one of the best routes to a feeling of wellbeing, but you can't give vent to a great guffaw if you are self-conscious about your teeth and breath.

If you visit a dentist regularly (every 6 months), clean your teeth properly (possibly with an electric toothbrush), and floss frequently (before you clean your teeth), you should encounter few problems. However, like every other part of your body, stress takes its toll on your teeth. Stress creates an acid environment in your mouth and evidence is mounting that the neurotoxic mercury continuously released from amalgam (mercury) fillings could be leading to allergies, headaches, fatigue syndromes and skin conditions. The alternative is to have them replaced with composite (plastic and ceramic) or porcelain fillings which not only alleviate related problems but also give you a confident all-white smile.

The future tooth

Marie Claire magazine (January 1998) reports that scientists are working on the process of 'curing' a tooth rather than drilling it out and refilling it. Growth factor is a chemical that occurs naturally in the body and signals cells in children's teeth to produce the hard substance, dentine. Once the second set of teeth has formed, the process becomes dormant. By reactivating it, it is already possible to grow new teeth in the laboratory. So the technology to regenerate your own teeth could one day be available in your dentist's chair.

Gums, tongues and breath

Gargle frequently with warm salt water to keep infections at bay and boost the circulation in your gums by massaging them with your fingertips and finely ground sea salt. Brushing your tongue as well as your teeth can help make the whole mouth feel cleaner and the breath fresher. There are tongue brushes on the market, but your own toothbrush is perfectly adequate.

An effective Asian tradition is to chew fennel and cardamom seeds after meals to help prevent tooth decay, gum disease and bad breath. Chewing parsley is also useful for freshening breath and getting rid of strong-smelling food such as garlic.

When wellbeing is tested

Your wellbeing can be affected in a great number of ways. Here are a few specific action points to help you get over the worst.

Acne

Acne is an extremely complex condition with a number of causes: overactive sebaceous glands, blocked sebaceous ducts, bacterial activity, inflammation in the surrounding tissue. Your genes largely determine whether you get it and how bad it is. It affects around 80 per cent of teenagers to different degrees and at least one woman in twenty has acne after the age of twenty-five. In its severe form, it is an extremely distressing condition that can cause psychological inhibitions and have a marked effect on the sufferer's wellbeing. Acne can increase stress and stress can exacerbate acne. In such cases, medical help is advised.

To help prevent acne, do what you can for your general good health – eating the right things, getting plenty of fresh air and exercise, using the right skin care products and, very importantly, tackle any anxieties to lower your stress levels. Washing is important to remove grime, surface oil, make-up and dead skin cells. Abrasive scrubs and mitts are not generally recommended as they can aggravate the condition. Chinese medicine can be effective and diluted tea tree oil is a good standby to dab on in the event of a breakout.

Acne healing mask

> **2 tsp honey**
> **¼ tsp fine sea salt**
> **1 tsp turmeric**

Mix to a thick paste and apply to clean skin. Leave on for at least 30 minutes or even overnight. Rinse off with warm water and pat the skin dry.

Cellulite

Cellulite is fat, but it is the way that the fat is distributed that gives it the form known as cellulite. It only affects women – around 95 per cent will have it to a greater or lesser extent and it can certainly be reduced if not shifted. Take the usual approach: good diet, exercise and massage, which is the basis of general good health. If the cellulite doesn't actually go, you will still feel fitter and full of energy.

Dry skin brushing is one of the best ways to treat cellulite and a sluggish circulation. It gives dull-looking skin a lift. The best time to do it is first thing in the morning before your bath or shower. Using a natural fibre body brush or sisal massage mitt, start on the soles of the feet, then use strong sweeping strokes up the legs, over the stomach, sides and chest and then finish with the arms. Always brush towards the heart following the flow of the lymphatic drainage system. This will help eliminate toxins and dramatically improve skin tone.

Puffy eyes

Puffy eyes are generally worse when you wake up, but often have nothing to do with actually being tired – you just look it. Hollywood legend says there are some stars who use haemorrhoid cream to treat under-eye puffiness. This is a very bad idea and will do no more (probably far less) good than applying an ice cube wrapped in a flannel. There is also the tea bag remedy, which is still much acclaimed. Strong teas such as Assam are said to be the best. Rinse the bags under the tap, put them in the refrigerator for half an hour, and then onto your eyes for about 20 minutes. For a more convenient pick-me-up for tired-looking eyes, use an eye gel which is instant and soothing in its effect.

Brittle nails

Great-looking hands and nails give valuable emphasis to expression, but nails that are a mess can be a distraction. The cuticle protects the tissue from which the nail is formed. It is vital not to damage this delicate area either by cutting, pushing it back too roughly or by using cuticle-destroying chemicals because you run the risk of introducing an infection which will deform your nails. Brittle and flaking nails are commonly due to contact with harsh soaps and detergents, and repeated immersion in water which swells and shrinks the nail structure – causing them eventually to split. Prevention is better than any cure in this case. Use rubber gloves to protect your hands and nails and moisturize around the nails with pure almond oil (see page 130). Nails give a strong indication of health, so if you have troublesome, brittle, cracked or flaky nails, it may be a good idea to show them to your doctor in case there is some underlying cause.

Smoking

The risks of heart and lung disease are well-documented. But in clinical studies, testers over-estimated the age of most long-term smokers by five to ten years. Smoking depletes your levels of vitamin C and damages the elastic tissue that keeps the skin tight. Squint lines develop around the eyes from trying to keep out the smoke and deeply etched lines form around the upper lip as a consequence of repeated drawing on the cigarette. Stopping smoking is possibly the single most important thing you can do to increase your sense of wellbeing. If you are determined to stop, there are plenty of groups who will give you advice and support. Decide exactly when and how you are going to do it and believe you can succeed.

Ageing skin

No matter what you do for yourself, you will one day have to face the signs of ageing. The best way to assess what will happen and when is to look at your parents. Your genetic inheritance is the most important factor in the process. How will you respond? In crisis or with philosophical calm?

Wrinkles fall naturally into the places where the skin is creased most often. Laughter lines form around the eyes and mouth, and frown lines between the brows – they all map a life story, and cosmetic surgery will only help to edit the truth.

Collagen implants, dermabrasion, surgery and injecting a paralysing drug into the forehead to prevent frowning and therefore wrinkles are really bizarre, expensive and invasive treatments which carry serious health risks. If our years of laughter and tears are etched into our memories and our faces, they should be treasured. Once we can appreciate our individual characteristics, we can simply make the best of what we've got – naturally.

wellbeing and the power of touch

Touch has become taboo in crowded Western societies where maintaining your space is a life's work. Too easily associated with invasion, aggression and abuse, touch is neglected as a fundamental human need.

Countless studies underline how vital touch is to both our mental and physical wellbeing. Early studies last century demonstrated that children who are frequently picked up and held thrive better and are more resistant to illness. In the 1930s, Dr René Spitz's American studies of orphans confirmed that babies may even die through lack of touch, and touch-deprived children that survive often become physically and mentally retarded. Recently, work at the Touch Research Institute at the University of Miami Medical School has found that a 30-minute neck massage can reduce depression, lower levels of the stress hormones cortisol and norepinephrine, improve alertness and raise the quality of sleep.

Throughout life, our craving for touch is chemical. There is growing evidence that skin is like a well-stocked pharmacy housing potent natural opiates, endorphins, for example, which have an analgesic effect. Massage is an instinctive pain reliever – if we hurt ourselves, we automatically 'rub it better'. According to Dr Peter Collett, a research psychologist at New College, Oxford, having our skin rubbed not only acts as a local anaesthetic, but stimulates the brain into releasing euphoric, morphine-like chemicals called enkephalins. Along with endorphins, they not only dull the pain, but can also help immunize against illness and disease. Scientists also believe that touch stimulates a surge of oxytocin, the highly addictive peptide and 'love' chemical. Not only does it contribute to the 'Velcro' effect of sexual and parental bonding, it actually increases our sensitivity to touch. It has also been used to treat depression, schizophrenia and obsessive-compulsive disorders.

interaction

Without constant touch, we risk becoming depressive, aggressive, less able to express affection or enjoy normal social interaction.

loving

In a therapy situation, unconditional loving touch – without sexual, manipulative or possessive connotation – is profoundly relaxing and reassuring.

massage

Basic massage, for example, can go beyond de-knotting tense muscles and lowering pulse rate and blood pressure.

affirmation

To a lonely or emotionally isolated person, re-established contact can be an affirmation of his or her self-worth.

perspective

If you have a problem you can't see around, holistic massage can give you a far more grounded sense of perspective. As well as relaxing you physically, it pulls all your energies back into place.

'Touch has stronger communication than the value of words', believes British massage expert Clare Maxwell-Hudson, who has organized teams of practitioners in NHS hospitals and teaches massage to students at the Royal College of Nursing in London. In addition to soothing pain and encouraging relaxation, she claims that there is evidence that people remember things more clearly if you touch them as you are talking to them.

Counsellor and nurse Jean-Sayre Adams is senior tutor of Therapeutic Touch (TT), a controversial, hands-on healing technique she brought from America for use in British hospitals. Over the past ten years, she has successfully trained around 1,500 nurses and health workers and has helped to establish TT as part of a complementary therapy degree programme for nurses and midwives at Manchester University. Also known as the Kreiger/Kunz Method, TT is based less on faith than quantum mechanics, a progressive school of physics that relates to universal cause and effect. It subscribes to the theory that illness is caused by blocks in the patient's energy field. Through a series of stroking movements, TT re-balances energy, relaxes the patient and allows their own 'life force' to do the healing.

Emotional rescue

The fact that touch is a powerful catalyst to emotional as well as physical release is a crucial aspect of progressive massage systems.

Earlier this century, psychoanalyst Wilhelm Reich, a student of Freud and a holistic visionary well ahead of his time, was among the first to air the idea that psychological trauma could be stored in bone and muscle. Reich believed that tissue has memory – traumatize it and each time that zone is touched, the memory of impact is released. The theory would seem to have some physiological basis. Pain messages from all areas of the body pass through the limbic system – the brain's emotional memory bank – on their way to the cerebral cortex. If you don't like being touched in a particular area, you could be subconsciously associating it with a traumatic past incident that your conscious mind has blocked. Likewise, a classic hunched, defensive, tense-shouldered posture may be causing chronic low self-esteem. Reichian massage evolved to release the underlying emotional cause through easing the muscular block and restoring the free-flow of orgone energy – his name for the life force.

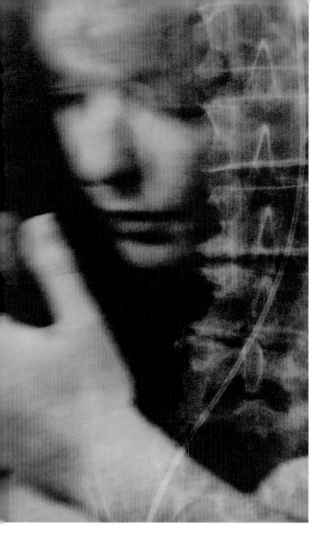

Gerda Boyesen, a Norwegian Manipulative Therapies psychologist and Reichian analyst who developed the technique known as biodynamics, also found that blocked energy builds up in the form of fluids trapped between muscles and nerves. Once the fluid is dispersed, spontaneous peristalsis in the intestine processes it. She likened this 'gut reaction' to the Chinese medicine concept that every organ has two functions – physical and esoteric, or 'meaningful'. Stress then, is meaningfully digested by the intestines – a now familiar theory to the lay person.

Reichian therapists listen to the intestines through stethoscopes as they work. To them, tummy rumblings, churnings and gurglings are positive signs that stress is being released and digested. A stress-free system, they say, sounds like a smoothly babbling brook.

Virtually all touch therapies seem to uphold Reich's theories on stress. There are countless anecdotes of spontaneous emotional releases like sobbing, laughing, or flashes of grief or anger as long-suppressed memories begin to surface. Many therapists also have counselling skills, or may recommend a course of 'talking therapy' for specific emotional problems. Some therapies are active catalysts that complement self-development. It's not unusual for therapists to combine some form of touch with talk. And if you're mortified because your stomach rumbles the moment you hit the couch, don't be. It's like music to your therapist's ears.

Since man discovered stress, healing massage has been key to traditional health philosophies the world over. In the 5th century BC, Hippocrates, the Greek 'father of medicine', declared that all physicians should be expert in 'rubbing' and that the key to health was a scented bath and an oiled massage daily. Seven thousand years later, touch therapy is an increasingly popular, hugely enjoyable way of maintaining health and preventing disease. These are some of your options.

Massage

Swedish massage

Good for: General relaxation and stress-busting. High blood pressure, depression, headaches, insomnia. Digestive problems like irritable bowel syndrome, constipation. Muscular and joint sprains, backache, arthritis, rheumatism, sciatica.

What it is: Kneading and stroking the skin and muscles with varying degrees of pressure to relax tense muscles and stimulate blood and lymph circulation. When the body is relaxed, its autonomic functions, including digestion and breathing, improve. For thousands of years, almost all cultures have practised some form of massage. But early last century, a Swedish gymnast, Per Henrik Ling, devised the formal technique based on anatomy which has become the basis for modern Western massage.

What happens: The practitioner uses a combination of movements in Swedish therapeutic massage. Effleurage or stroking improves circulation, relaxes tense muscles and soothes nerves. Slow movements calm, brisk movements stimulate. Petrissage or kneading with fingers and thumbs stretches and relaxes tense muscles and improves circulation, absorption of nutrients via the bloodstream and elimination of waste matter. Light kneading affects skin and the top layer of muscles; deep kneading affects deeper muscles. Tapotement or percussion – pummelling with loose fists or hacking with the sides of the hands – usually happens at the end of a massage and is invigorating, stimulating and awakening.

In addition, deep thumb or knuckle pressures release specific muscular tension or 'knots' especially on pressure points at nerve, muscle and bone junctions.

Holistic massage

Good for: Stress-busting in general or during traumatic life phases, such as bereavement and divorce. Holistic massage can also be used as a personal development aid in conjunction with counselling or psychotherapy.

What it is: A massage that releases emotional stress stored in tissue and muscle tension. Following increasing anecdotes of emotional responses and trauma recall during basic Swedish massage, studies found that different emotions relate to specific body areas. Anger accumulates in the shoulders, grief in the chest, and fear in the lower back and kidneys, for example. Like biodynamic massage, holistic massage evolved to deal specifically with this mind-body feedback.

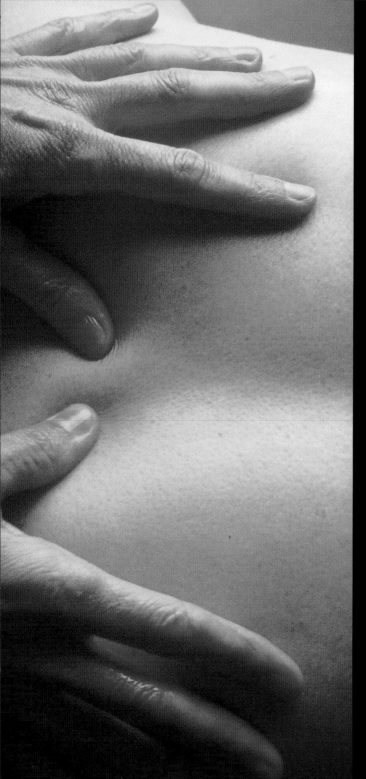

What happens: First the therapist massages the entire body to check out the patient's physical and emotional state. Then specific tensions are worked on. Techniques used are eclectic, and range from featherlight to deep touch.

Treatments are intuitive and tailored to the patient's needs. The therapist may also include techniques from other therapies, like cranio-sacral or hands-on healing. When a release occurs, patients often sob, laugh, yawn or sigh the stress out of their system. Therapists usually have counselling skills to help deal with the fall-out.

'It's an excellent mind and body treatment which can prove transformational', says Elaine Williams, head of natural therapies at a British health farm where holistic massage is among the most popular treatments. 'If you have a problem that you can't see your way around, it can give you a far more grounded sense of perspective. As well as relaxing you physically, it pulls all your energies back into place.'

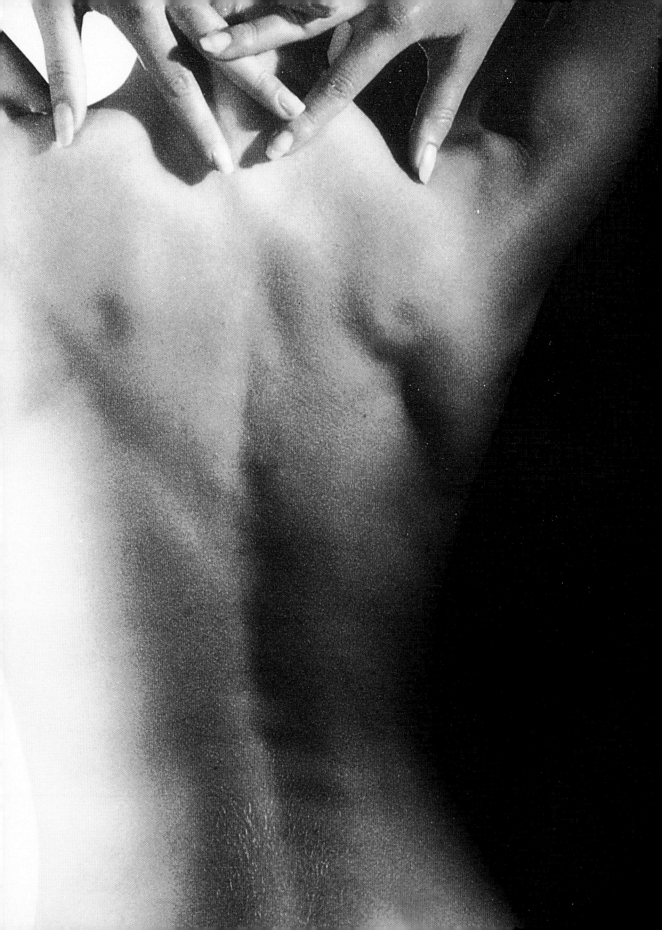

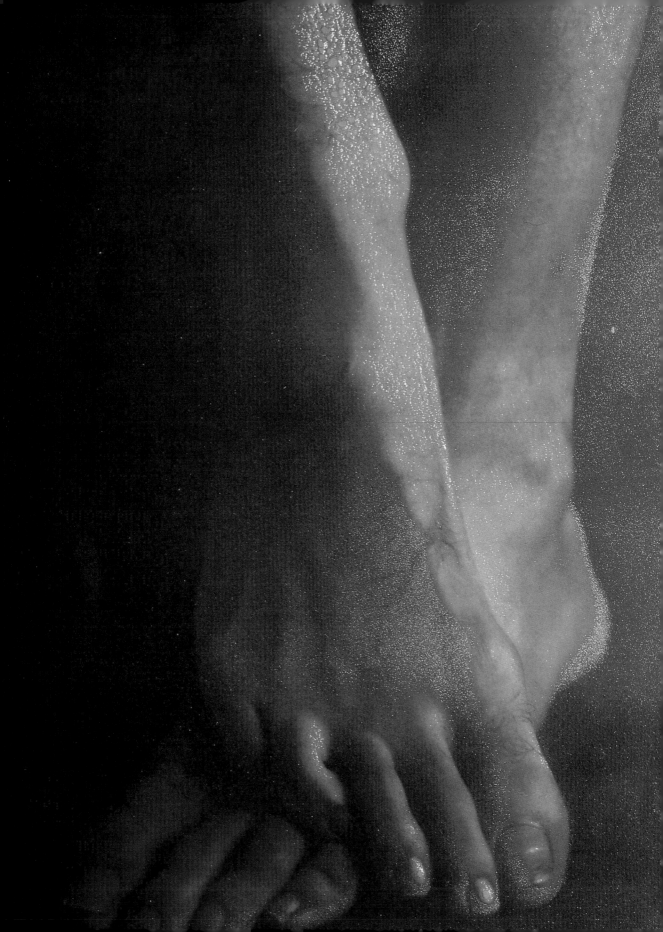

Reflexology

Good for: Health and energy maintenance. Problems with digestion, constipation. Fluid retention, like swollen legs and puffy ankles. Menstrual bloating, cramps and irregularities. Menopausal symptoms. Stress, fatigue and migraines. Skin problems.

What it is: A technique of treating the entire body by massaging reflex points in the foot and occasionally the hands. Foot massage is ancient – an Egyptian tomb painting shows it being done. Modern reflexology dates back to 1902, when American ear, nose and throat specialist Dr William Fitzgerald introduced 'zone therapy'. Echoing the Chinese philosophy of meridians or energy channels, Fitzgerald theorized that the body's energy flowed along ten zones from the head and ending in reflex points in the feet and hands. He found that, because all parts of the body are linked by these zones, pressing one area could produce an anaesthetic or healing effect in another. Physiotherapist Eunice Ingham took his theories further by maintaining that all

parts of the body, including internal organs, could be treated by manipulating points on the feet alone.

What happens: Reflexology owes its huge popularity partly to its non-invasiveness – only the bare feet are manipulated while you lie back fully clothed. The therapist applies firm finger and thumb pressure over the sole and around the heels and ankles. Imagine your big toe is your head, your instep is your waistline and your heel is the base of your spine. By stimulating relevant points, the therapist eases tension, dissolves blockages and boosts the circulation of energy, blood and lymph to and from the organs. Reflexologists say that congestion feels like granular crystals underneath the skin, which they aim to break down and disperse. To you, the zone may feel sensitive, ranging from mildly tingling to downright sore. Afterwards, you'll either feel like running a marathon or crawling under the duvet. You may also perspire or need to go to the toilet more, since reflexology stimulates toxic elimination. Most people feel the full benefits the day after.

Bodywork

Osteopathy

Good for: Back and joint pain, aches and strains. Rheumatism, arthritis, sports injuries, PMS and asthma.

What it is: Founded in the 1870s by American doctor Andrew Taylor Still, osteopathy deals not only with bones, but the tendons, ligaments and muscles that hold them in place and allow them to move. In a healthy, musculo-skeletal system, all these elements interact smoothly. Poor posture, a lifetime of carrying or lifting heavy loads, repetitive strain or injury can throw the system out of balance, overloading certain areas, compromising others and causing restricted mobility and pain. Cranial osteopathy was developed at the turn of the century by Still's student, William Garner Sutherland, who believed that if the bones in the skull are knocked out of position, their subtle movements are impaired. This restricts cranial rhythm impulses (CRI) which affects other body functions. Gentle manipulation eases the cranial bones back into place and restores optimum CRI. Cranial osteopathy should not be confused with cranio-sacral therapy, below.

What happens: It is the osteopath's job to relieve the strain by systematic massage and manipulation. Forget the bone-crunching image of osteopathy. For the record, that almost sickening 'crack' is due to air compression joints – not the splintering of bones. Surprisingly, it is both painless and pain-relieving. But practitioners these days prefer not to use the 'cracking' high-velocity thrusts to reposition joints. Instead, they are more likely to ease them back into place through positioning and supporting the body in a series of rhythmic movements and deep stretches.

Nevertheless, osteopathy can be a tender affair. Practitioners prod or 'palpate' tissues, muscles and joints to test their temperature, tension, shape and reflex. They also check your standing, sitting and lying down posture to determine the origins of the imbalance. Occasionally, they may arrange X-rays and blood tests. Most prescribe stretches and exercises to do at home between treatments, to strengthen, improve mobility and help re-educate your stance.

Chiropractic

Good for: Spine and neck injuries, whiplash. Arm and shoulder pain, lower back pain. Stress, migraine, asthma, tinnitus, vertigo. Digestive problems, constipation and painful periods.

What it is: A form of manipulation similar to osteopathy, although the

technique differs slightly. Chiropractors concentrate more on the spine and frequently use X-rays to detect imbalances. Because the spinal column protects the central nervous system, a nerve trapped between vertebrae can cause problems elsewhere in the body. With its name derived from the Greek 'cheiro', or hand, and 'praktikos', or practice, chiropractic was developed by a Canadian osteopath, David Daniel Palmer in 1895 who restored an employee's hearing by correcting his spinal and neck injury. Chiropractic had controversial beginnings in the US, but is now an accepted therapy recommended by doctors on both sides of the Atlantic. In 1990, a study by a Medical Research Council team reported in the *British Medical Journal* found that chiropractic treatment had improved patients' conditions by 70 per cent more than regular hospital out-patient care that had been given to a control group.

What happens: The first session is usually diagnostic – your posture is checked and X-rays may be taken. Then treatment begins for real. As you sit, stand or lie on the couch, the practitioner slowly mobilizes the relevant vertebra as far as it will go, then quickly thrusts it even further. This sudden stretching extends and relaxes muscular spasms. Because it catches you unawares before you have had a chance to tense against it, the

'unlocking' of a joint is relatively pain free. Relief can be immediate, although you may feel a bit sore and stiff a few hours later. If your problem is severe, follow-up chiropractic sessions may be necessary.

Cranio-sacral therapy

Good for: Headaches, migraine, sinus problems. Stress and posture-related shoulder and back pain.

What it is: Devised by American osteopath Dr John Upledger, cranio-sacral therapy is an offshoot of cranial osteopathy which uses extremely subtle manipulation to free tension between the bones of the head and spine. The cranio-sacral system includes the bones of the cranium (top of the head) and sacrum (base of the spine); the brain and spinal cord membranes which contain cerebro-spinal fluid; and the fibrous tissue, or fascia connecting the muscles. This system has an energy with its own subtle pulse. Tension blocks within it can affect the entire body, as every organ, muscle and tissue group is linked by nerves to precise points on the cranio-sacral system. Similarly, feedback from a stiff limb joint can upset the subtle cranio-sacral circulation and throw the body off-balance.

The touch may be feather light, but it's deeply relaxing. There is no pulling, forcing or even massage. Therapists believe that the body tenses in defence against rough handling, and yields more readily to subtle coaxing. Their role is to simply support the head, spine and occasionally other zones and allow tension to uncoil. It's as if the body has its own self-healing urges and only needs permission to go with them.

According to Thomas Atlee, Principal of the College of Cranio-Sacral Therapy in London, every tension, injury and illness – both physical and mental – leaves its mark. The therapist can feel restrictions and the body pulling subtly against them. 'By giving the body freedom to go its natural way, you get to the point of release', he says.

What happens: It is truly amazing how profound the effects of this subtle treatment can be. It's not unusual to feel as though you're floating above the couch, or that your body is turning from left to right as tensions uncoil and energies find their pathways again. There is also something very special about just being held, or supported. Often you can't help laughing, weeping or simply yawning and sighing with the relief of it all. At the end of a successful session, you feel refreshed and pleasantly expanded. An important part of cranio-sacral work is with babies and children. Therapists recommend that infants are checked within six months of birth to ensure

the soft platelets in their skull have recovered from compression in the birth canal or from forceps during a breach birth. It is these compressions imposing on areas of the brain that may prove the cause of behavioural problems and glue ear, as well as headaches, migraine or sinus conditions in adult life. Babies who are treated sleep and eat better and seem better adjusted. So do grown-ups – it's never too late to start treatment.

Bowen technique

Good for: Sports and lower back injuries. Tension headaches. Asthma. Stomach problems, constipation and incontinence.

What it is: A very simple, gentle form of manipulation that works on the fascia, or the muscles' connective tissue, this therapy was originated by Tom Bowen, an Australian medical student who became an industrial chemist after service in World War Two.With no formal training behind him, by 1950 he had devised his own eclectic form of therapy involving specific bodywork movements and natural home remedies. His system became so popular – by 1974 he was treating an estimated 13,000 patients a year – that the Australian federal government felt they had to investigate him. Amazingly they found that his success rate was 80-90 per cent after one or two treatments. This success continues to defy analysis. Bowen never explained exactly how his technique worked and his secret died with him in 1982. But Oswald Rentsch who studied his technique and later taught it to others describes it as being based on the theory that energy is trapped in various body zones, causing disharmony and disease. Once the energy is freed, the body can begin healing itself.

What happens: The Bowen Technique is concerned with bringing about changes in the body that in turn lead to self-healing. As you lie on the couch, therapists work over the body in a series of light rolling hand movements, described as being like rolling a ball up a hill, then nudging it over the top. Like cranio-sacral therapy, the moves are so light and subtle, it's hard to believe they'll work. But practitioners believe they are 'communicating' with

the body, coaxing it back into balance so that it can work properly. Oddly, you can either feel exuberantly energized and marvellously stretched and flexible after a treatment – or worse. But since some kind of change has inevitably taken place, relief often follows a day or two later. The practitioner may also give you basic home care advice. Epsom salt baths are recommended for arthritis, bunions and cancer. Washing soda compresses ease swollen joints; and cider vinegar and honey drinks soothe rheumatism.

Polarity therapy

Good for: Balancing health and energy. Migraine, digestive problems, allergies, ME, back pain and sciatica.

What it is: A total balancing system that uses bodywork, nutrition, exercise and counselling. Founded at the beginning of the century in the US by Randolph Stone, the system, reminiscent of Ayurveda and traditional Chinese medicine, is based on the theory that the body is like a living magnet, with energy currents flowing back and forth between positive and negative poles. A well-regulated flow means optimum health; blockages mean illness and disease.

What happens: Part of the initial counselling involves making a note of everything you eat and drink for five or so days, to help the therapist gauge your energy balance. Bodywork is like a combination of osteopathy, reflexology and Indian massage, with firm acupressure and joint manipulation. For energy balancing, the right side of the body is regarded as positive and the left negative. The therapist also uses her right hand to stimulate and the left to soothe, while gently rocking or shaking body zones to boost energy flow. Polarity yoga consists of poses designed to calm or stimulate; and dietary advice includes plenty of fresh fruit and vegetable juices, plus cleansing regimes. Talking is part of the therapy that helps disperse emotional blockages.

Zero balancing

Good for: Neck and back pain, stress, migraine and sports injuries.

What it is: A combination of hands-on healing and energy balancing developed in the 1970s by physician, acupuncturist and osteopath Dr Fritz Smith. Zero balancing aims to soothe, stretch and balance both physical and mental energies and provide mind, body and soul healing. Theoretically, the body has three energy fields – an aura-like background energy, a worldly vertical energy which gives us a sense of space, and an internal energy circulation. This internal flow has a further three subdivisions. The deepest circulates through bone, the middle through muscles, nerves, blood and

organs, and the superficial level controls the sweat glands and skin. Physical and emotional traumas can affect any of these subtle energy circulations. Zero balancing therefore clears blocks and eases the flow.

What happens: Before training, practitioners must be qualified in other bodyworking areas, like osteopathy, acupuncture or physiotherapy. Manipulation is bone-deep and covers the entire body, with the practitioner supporting, rotating and stretching limbs and joints. Often physical manipulation releases emotional memory, which may be the underlying cause of stress, although unlike other therapies, you don't have to talk if you don't want to.

Alexander technique

Good for: Anxiety, arthritis, asthma, lower back pain, depression, fatigue, stiff neck and shoulders, stomach ulcers, high blood pressure, repetitive strain injury (RSI), breathing disorders, headaches, gynaecological problems.

What it is: A postural new way of life. This system teaches how to sit, stand and move efficiently and gracefully without straining any area of your body. It was devised in the late nineteenth century by Australian actor Frederick Matthias Alexander, who unaccountably lost his voice. When he studied himself in the mirror, he

One of the best-learned postural movements is how to lift objects correctly. Always bend your knees and, keeping your back straight, rise to standing using your legs to push you up and without twisting your spine. Do it this way and you will not put unnecessary strain on the back.

noticed that before he spoke, he habitually jerked back his head so that his throat muscles tightened visibly. He trained himself not to jerk and tense, and his voice was restored. He also found both his physical and emotional health improved. From childhood onwards, like Alexander, we all develop constricting postural habits that limit our full health potential. Stiff joints, shallow breathing, restricted circulation and back ache and the classic 'dowager's hump' are common symptoms of this sedentary age of hunching over keyboards. Poor posture often has psychological links – depressed people tend to collapse into themselves and people rarely keep their 'chin up'.

What happens: An Alexander session is usually on a one-to-one, teacher-pupil basis. During the first session, your standing, walking, sitting and lying postures are assessed, while the teacher gently guides you into optimum positions that your body will eventually learn. The popular conception of the Alexander technique is having to repeat over and over again the correct way of getting up and sitting down. It takes your body a lifetime to learn bad habits, so unlearning them takes practice. But since the rewards are looking taller and more slender and feeling more supple, it's worth all the studied repetition.

Hellerwork/Rolfing

Good for: Improving posture and mobility. Easing injuries and releasing trapped emotions. Personal growth.

What it is: Deep-reaching, restructuring and rebalancing bodywork developed by Joseph Heller, who believed that psychological trauma is held in the muscles and fascia, or tissues that envelop them. Poor posture, for example, may result from low self-esteem, characterized by hunched shoulders. Hellerwork concentrates on de-hunching the body and freeing the

negative emotions that constrain it. Similar to hellerwork, rolfing or 'postural integration' is a system of deep massage and manipulation of connective tissue and muscles that realigns the body on a straight, vertical line. The earth's gravity field can then support the body's energy field and our self-healing powers function fully. Rolfing was developed in the 1940s by Dr Ida Rolf, an American biochemist, who discovered that the fascia, or connective tissue that keeps bones and muscles in place, adapt to support postural habits, no matter how bad. Stretching them back again restores balance.

What happens: Enthusiasts say you can grow inches taller through hellerwork or rolfing. Each session concentrates on a different body zone and the emotion it carries. The concurrent release enables both physical and emotional expansion. But the manipulation can be painful and sometimes feel invasive. It requires trust. It's not easy to allow someone to ease their fingertips under your ribcage and gently pull upwards. Breathing through it certainly helps. It could be said that hellerwork and rolfing helps you give birth to a 'new you'. Stick with the course which works through the body zones in sequence, and you could be rewarded with renewed vitality and confidence as well as a well-balanced skeleton.

Hands-on, energy and spiritual healing

Shiatsu

Good for: Backaches, neck aches, stress-related disorders, encouraging positive emotional feelings.

What it is: Oriental medicine is based on the idea that everything has a subtle flow of electro-magnetic energy running through it. This energy is called *chi* in China, *ki* in Japan, and *prana* in India. It carries your thoughts and emotions around your body, moving along 14 'meridians' which branch out until every cell in your body is affected by whatever you are thinking or feeling. Along each meridian are points, called tsubos, where the flow of ki can be most easily influenced. Each tsubo potentially improves the flow of ki that relates to a specific kind of problem.

You can alter the flow of *ki* with yoga, t'ai chi, acupuncture or the massage technique called shiatsu. Shiatsu is an intimate therapy because the practitioner uses his or her body and *ki* energy to bring about a change in yours. This is what makes it such a powerful form of healing. There are many kinds, some using deep pressure, others focusing on gently holding tsubos, to subtly alter the flow of *ki*.

What happens: Typically lasting for 60-90 minutes, a shiatsu treatment combines careful pressure on various tsubos with long, slow stretches. Also included in shiatsu are techniques common in massage, such as kneading tight muscles, pounding, rocking the body to loosen joints and increasing movement of joints. Some practitioners will also use a form of hands-on healing to project their own ki energy into their patient's body.

Many of the techniques require you to be on a solid surface, so you may be asked to sit or lie on a futon. To have a shiatsu, you normally wear loose cotton clothing. Shiatsu is not normally applied directly to the skin and any kind of synthetic clothing will upset the practitioner's ability to influence the flow of your *ki* energy.

Shiatsu at home

There are many tsubos you can work on yourself. In most cases, the trick is to locate the tsubo, breath in and press into the tsubo with your thumb as you slowly breath out. You will need to repeat this for three to ten minutes to notice any benefit. It is then good practice to work on the same tsubo on the other side of your body. The following tsubos are listed by their meridian and the number of the tsubo from the beginning of the meridian.

Large intestine four
Used for: Headaches, toothache, neck tension and constipation.
Location: Slide your finger along the bone between the knuckle of your index finger and the joint where the bones from your index finger and thumb join. About halfway along, you will feel a small indentation in the bone. You should feel a sharp pain here.
Technique: Press into the fleshy mound next to the indentation. Rub firmly to release endorphins and release pain. Concentrate on the hand that is most sensitive. Alternatively, press and hold to help with constipation. Repeat on your other hand.

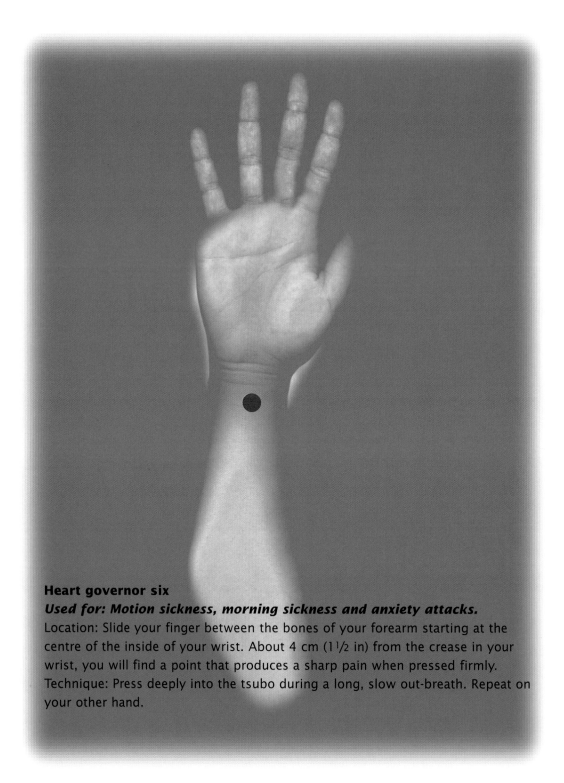

Heart governor six
Used for: Motion sickness, morning sickness and anxiety attacks.
Location: Slide your finger between the bones of your forearm starting at the centre of the inside of your wrist. About 4 cm (1 1/2 in) from the crease in your wrist, you will find a point that produces a sharp pain when pressed firmly.
Technique: Press deeply into the tsubo during a long, slow out-breath. Repeat on your other hand.

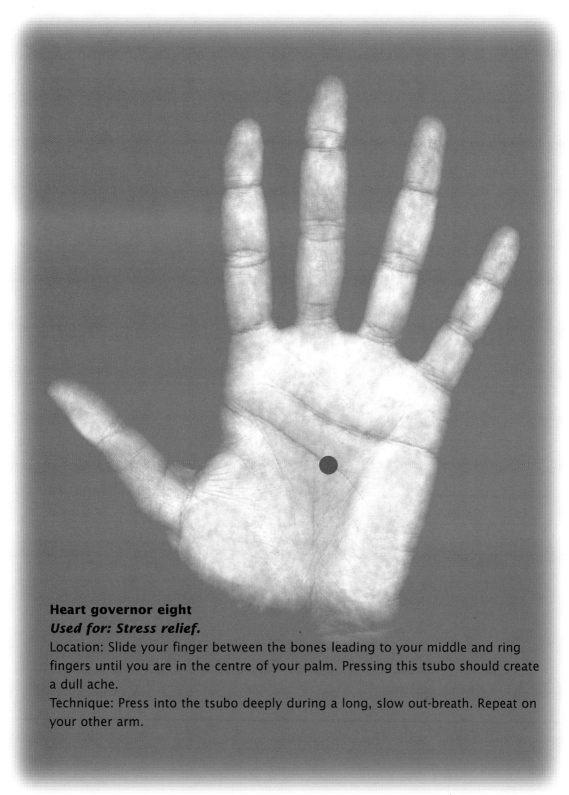

Heart governor eight
Used for: Stress relief.

Location: Slide your finger between the bones leading to your middle and ring fingers until you are in the centre of your palm. Pressing this tsubo should create a dull ache.

Technique: Press into the tsubo deeply during a long, slow out-breath. Repeat on your other arm.

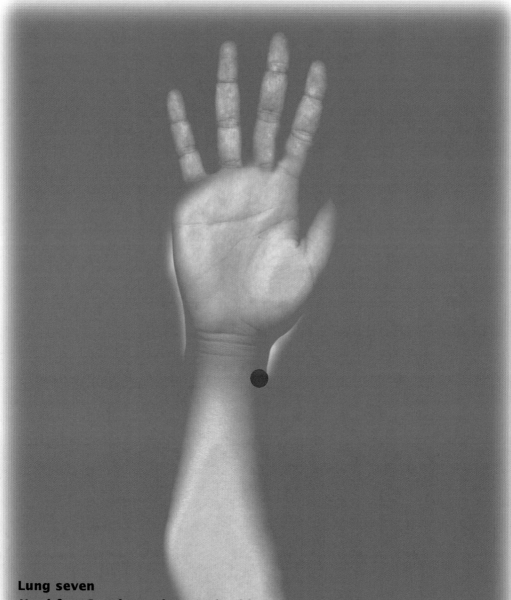

Lung seven
Used for: Coughs, asthma and colds.
Location: Place your little finger on the opposite wrist where the base of your thumb joins your arm. Keep your fingers together along the inside of the bone of your forearm. Press into the inside of the bone with your thumb. Slide 1 cm (3/8 in) up and down the bone until you find a particularly sensitive point.
Technique: press into the tsubo deeply during a long, slow out-breath. Repeat on your other arm.

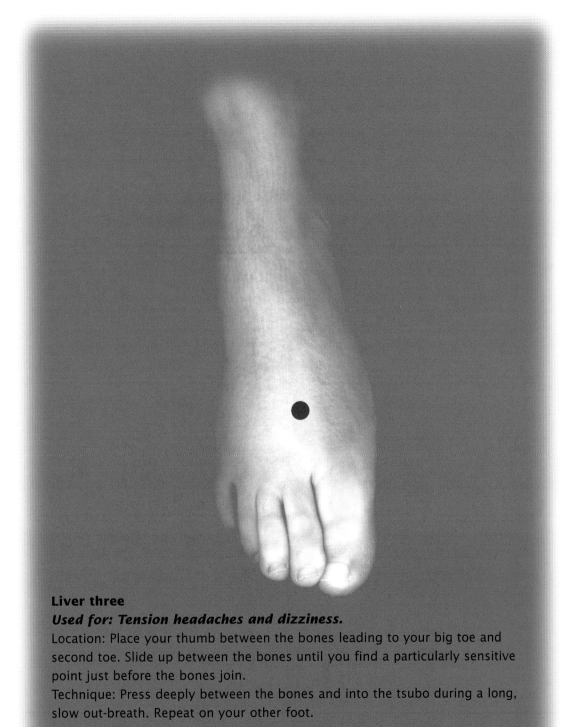

Liver three
Used for: Tension headaches and dizziness.
Location: Place your thumb between the bones leading to your big toe and
second toe. Slide up between the bones until you find a particularly sensitive
point just before the bones join.
Technique: Press deeply between the bones and into the tsubo during a long,
slow out-breath. Repeat on your other foot.

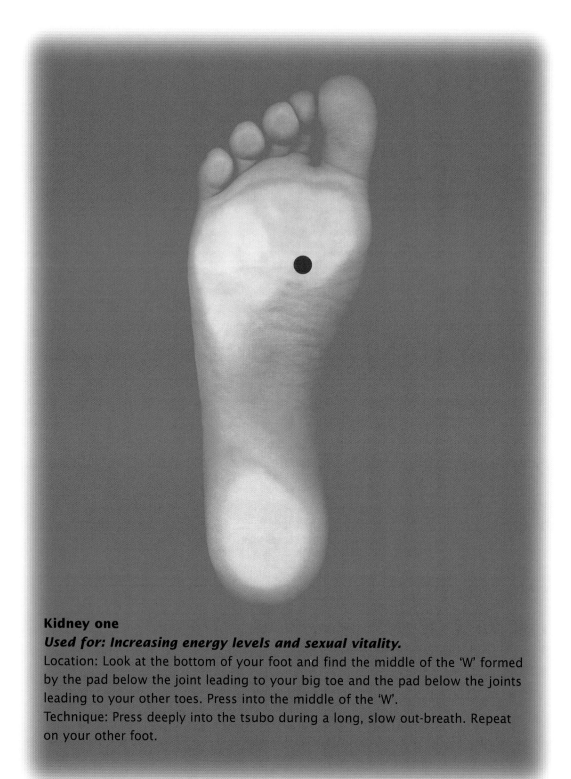

Kidney one
Used for: Increasing energy levels and sexual vitality.
Location: Look at the bottom of your foot and find the middle of the 'W' formed by the pad below the joint leading to your big toe and the pad below the joints leading to your other toes. Press into the middle of the 'W'.
Technique: Press deeply into the tsubo during a long, slow out-breath. Repeat on your other foot.

Reiki

Good for: Relaxation. Muscle strain, general aches and pains. Immune-related conditions like ME and HIV. Reiki is also a powerful self-development tool.

What it is: This hands-on healing system is one of the fastest growing therapies in the West. It takes relatively little time to learn, is easy to practise and has no undesirable side effects. It does however require faith. Developed in the mid-1800s by Dr Mikao Usui, Reiki loosely means the free flow of universal energy or *ki* – the Japanese *chi*. Usui was a Japanese theologian who resolved to fully understand the essence of spiritual healing, as taught in all the world's major philosophies. His eclectic system owes much to the Tibetan sutras or Buddhist texts. During meditative quests, symbols were revealed to him as the keys to tapping into the universal healing force. Reiki masters use these secret symbols to initiate their students, who are then opened as conductors for universal energy.

Practitioners believe that Reiki has a balancing effect on the body – a theory that seems to have been borne out by an independent study reported in the *American Journal of Holistic Nursing* in 1989. This study compared the blood counts of students before and after initiation. Over half the students showed increased haemoglobin and the rest a decrease. Nevertheless, Reiki makes no claims of miracle cures. Instead, it promotes a greater awareness and respect both for a higher life force and one's self. Reiki students are encouraged to treat themselves daily to bring balance into their spiritual lives as well as tending any physical problems. British Reiki Master Margaret-Ann Pauffley sees this as learning to love yourself, warts and all. 'We touch others with love, but we don't normally pay ourselves that respect', she says. 'It's extraordinary to focus on different body parts without thinking "my stomach's too big" or "my boobs are too small". It goes way beyond the physical. You're just nurturing and being there for yourself.'

What happens: The practitioner places their hands for up to ten minutes at a time over the entire head and body, front and back. Individual areas can also be treated – a painful joint, say, or an aching head. What the patient usually feels is deep warmth. Tingling sensations or gentle pulses of energy are also common. A treatment

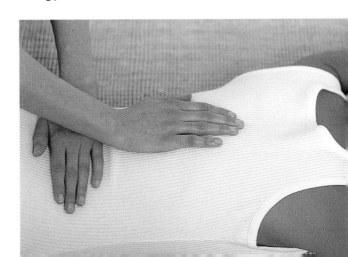

can be profoundly relaxing or energizing, depending on what your body needs. Pain is often relieved, but where inflammation is present, a temporary 'flare up' is by no means unusual before the throbbing subsides.

Metamorphic technique

Good for: Relaxation and personal development. Helping you to face major life changes or cope with chronic illness.

What it is: An extremely light, subtle form of massage that concentrates first on the feet, then hands and lastly, the head. Developed in the 1960s by British naturopath and reflexologist Robert St John, metamorphic technique derives its name from its ability to encourage a positive approach to take creative steps that change your life for the better. Since the foetus develops the head first and then the spine, St John believed that the spinal reflexes of the foot reflect the body's physical and psychic development from the moment before conception to eventual birth. In the womb, 'pre-natal patterns' establish emotional, physical and mental patterns that influence our wellbeing and susceptibility to disease in later life. Stimulating the spinal reflexes releases pre-birth trauma and negative self-conceptions and makes way for positive change.

What happens: Practitioners call themselves 'catalysts' – it's the body's own healing energies that do the real work. They help release energy blocks by using light circular massage movements, starting at the centre of the top of the big toe, moving down the inside edge of the foot to the mid-heel. They also work the 'emotional arch' that runs over the foot from ankle to ankle. Next the hands are massaged in a similar pattern from thumb tip to 'heel' and over the wrists; then the head is treated from the centre of the crown down and outwards along the base of the skull to either ear.

Metamorphic technique is so simple, it's learned in a weekend. Yet it is strangely effective and very, very popular. It can be done watching television, on children and adults alike. It is said that children with learning difficulties respond particularly well to its relaxing effects. It can also help to bring relief to terminally ill patients and their loved ones, as it's easy to give at a bedside, when there is precious little else you can do.

Crystal therapy

Good for: Balancing energies, healing injuries. Dispelling negatively charged atmospheres and encouraging positive thought.

What it is: The idea that semi-precious and precious stones can be used to heal is thousands of years old. The ancient Chinese used jade to treat kidney and bladder problems, and the American Indians were given stones at birth which would help strengthen both spiritual and physical fibre. Chosen according to colour and clarity or opaqueness, there is a stone that relates to virtually every human condition. Quartz and amethyst crystals, for example, are both considered universal 'cure alls' which can also amplify other healing methods.

What happens: Either placed on or around the body, crystals can be used to intensify the effects of hands-on healing or massage. Some give out energy, others are thought to absorb pain. They can also be used to channel energy. Ex-science teacher Harry Oldfield uses electromagnetic fields to amplify crystals in his electro-crystal therapy, designed to re-tune the body's natural vibrations. An X-ray-like camera scans the body for high frequency light waves, which indicate states of energy flow. These are then relayed to a computer screen for diagnosis. If the swirling areas of colour reveal blocked or weak energy zones, electromagnetic fields are beamed at these trouble spots to rejuvenate the zones. Gems can leave their energy blueprint in sunlit water, which is then taken as a therapeutic essence, rather like Bach flower remedies (see pages 191-2). Placed near a computer, quartz crystals help reduce static, offset radiation and improve concentration. They are also a useful focal point for meditation. But the most popular way of using gems is to wear them as protective talismans next to the skin.

智慧

Ancient wisdom, modern wellbeing

The Eastern approach to wellbeing has always been to maintain optimum health – not merely cure disease. Traditional holistic systems embrace physical, emotional and spiritual discipline – to follow them effectively is a way of life. In the West, they are attracting attention as often succeeding where mainstream medicine fails. The two following ancient medical philosophies have also influenced the many diverse complementary therapies that continue to evolve.

Traditional Chinese medicine (TCM)

Good for: Skin problems, especially eczema. Digestive disorders. Menstrual and menopausal problems. Chronic fatigue and ME.

What it is: An estimated 5,000 years old, TCM is a complete health system including diet, exercise, acupuncture and herbal remedies all employed to maintain yin/yang energy balance and facilitate the circulation of *chi*, or life force, through the meridians, or subtle energy channels.

There are 12 regular meridians. They run down the body in pairs, six on either side. They are named for the organs they run through. A disturbance in a meridian can cause an illness anywhere along that meridian. Toothache, for example, may be caused by an upset in the Stomach meridian, which passes through the upper gums. There is no better illustration of the holistic principle that is fundamental to TCM.

What happens: The peak flow of *chi* relies on the correct balance of the passive, feminine energy yin and active

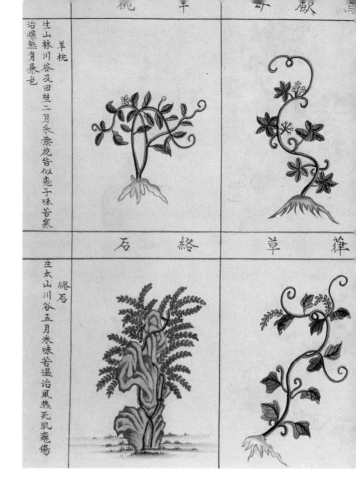

masculine energy yang present in all of us, whether male or female. Yin and yang are subdivided into eight principal patterns including hot and cold, or empty and full, which indicate bodily imbalances underlying potential disease. Hot symptoms, for example could be a red face, needing cooling foods and herbs; while cold could present as a slow pulse and pale tongue, requiring stimulating treatment. Emotional problems are also addressed. Ancient texts say that strong emotions can attack associated body organs. Joy and shock affect the heart; anger weakens the liver, and grief injures the lungs, for example. Five cosmic elements also govern our wellbeing. Fire, earth, air or metal, water and wood influence our personality and physical health. Too much of one element can tip our finely-tuned energy scales. Practitioners diagnose the imbalance, then prescribe the treatment most appropriate to re-establishing optimum *chi*.

TCM's best known therapy is acupuncture which stimulates chi flow by dispersing energy blocks. Needles are inserted into the surface skin over energy tapping points along the meridians, linked to specific organs, body zones and functions. A herb called moxa (mugwort) is sometimes burned on the tip of the needle, so that the heat travels downwards to warm the acupressure point and make it more receptive to treatment. This is especially effective where there is back or joint pain. Acupuncture has also claimed success in the treatment of migraines, asthma, arthritis, headaches and toothaches. The treatment is surprisingly bloodless and mostly painless, although on a bad day, it can be agony too. Reputable acupuncturists use disposable needles to maintain scrupulous hygiene.

Chinese herbalism hit the headlines in Britain when a trial at the Great Ormond Street Hospital for Sick Children showed that certain herbs were effective at treating some types of eczema. According to a report in the

medical journal *The Lancet*, treatment of malaria with Chinese herbs also looks promising. Chinese research indicates that herbs can reduce the symptoms of the HIV virus and in the USA, they are now being used to fight AIDS. Chinese herbalism is often used in conjunction with acupuncture to counteract the side effects of chemotherapy in cancer patients and there are ongoing studies into the use of herbs in controlling asthma, migraine and irritable bowel syndrome. Chinese herbs often taste so disgusting, you believe they must do good. But prescribed in the wrong dose by untrained practitioners, some herbs are toxic and can cause liver and kidney damage. It is therefore imperative to consult a qualified practitioner and follow their instructions to the letter.

Popular stress-busting exercises that boost *chi* circulation include t'ai chi and qi gong (see page 100). Both use a sequence of slow, graceful movements and breath control to calm, relax and energize the system. Practised by millions daily in China, it's said that t'ai chi harmonizes the body with the earth's energy field. It certainly serves to sharpen both the concentration and reflexes.

Ayurveda

Good for: Rebalancing your lifestyle for general health maintenance and stress control. Treating specific complaints that fail to respond to orthodox medicine. Ayurveda is often used to treat conditions including cardiovascular disease, arthritis, rheumatism, asthma, allergies, cancer, metabolic and digestive problems, skin disorders and viruses.

What it is: India's ancient, traditional medicine and philosophy system, embracing all aspects of wellbeing from nutrition and exercise to mental health and spiritual balance. Sometimes called 'the mother of all medicine', it is at least 3,000 years old.

What happens: Ayurveda works on the principle that it is possible to live perfectly healthily for 100 years hence its reputation as an anti-ageing system. The key to health lies in the body's balance of three major energy types, or *gunas*. *Sattvas* are wise and unifying energies; *rajas* are active; and *tamas* are passive.

Externally, we are also governed by five cosmic elements, called *doshas*. Earth relates to the body's solids like bones; water to fluids and soft tissue; fire to heat, digestion and metabolism; air to sensation and the nervous system; and ether to the body's networks and channels like veins and arteries. The *tridoshas* are derived from the five elements and subdivided into the body's bio-energies. *Pitta* generates heat and governs metabolism; *kapha* governs growth and structure, and *vata* generates all bodily movement. These three bio-energies also influence our *prakriti* or body type with its characteristic strengths and vulnerabilities.

Diet is an important aspect of Ayurveda and is used to correct imbalances in the doshas. Different food groups have their own light, passionate or sluggish qualities and can influence physical energy as well as subtle emotion. Herbs may be prescribed for specific illnesses. As well as diet, hygiene and massage, meditation and exercise make Ayurveda a holistic, balanced discipline. Its best-known mind/body workout is, of course, yoga. Massage traditionally uses warm oils to relax and rebalance. To perform *chavutti thirumal*, a deep massage technique from southern India, the therapist uses ropes to support and modulate their weight, while their feet massage and stroke your entire body, including your face.

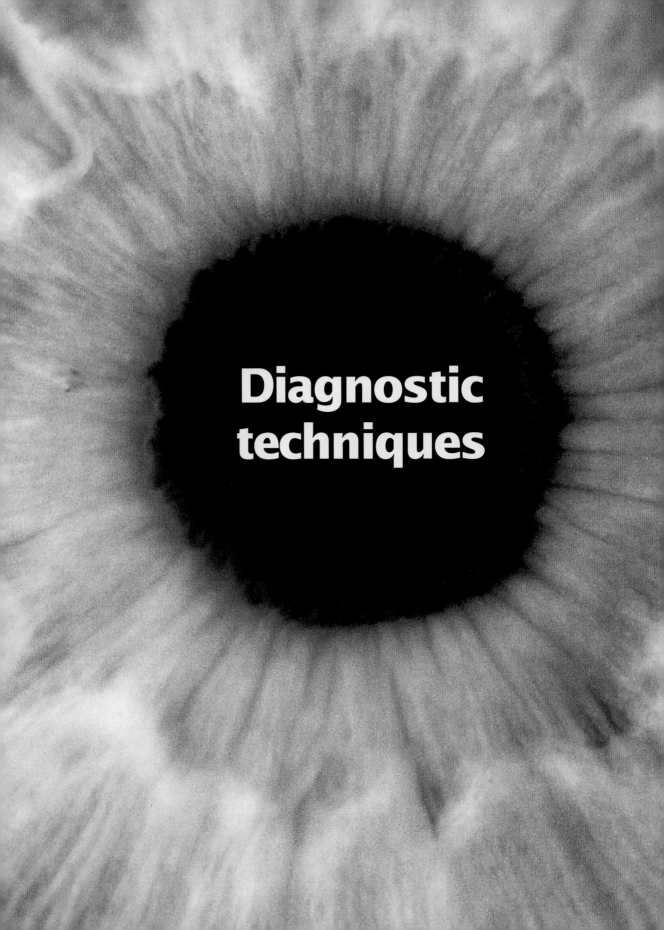

Diagnostic techniques

Iridology

Good for: Identifying physical and emotional disorders.

What it is: A diagnostic method which analyses the irides, or irises of the eyes, developed during the last century by Ignatz von Peczely, a Hungarian physician. Iridologists claim that the whole body is reflected by the eyes, because it is here that the entire nervous system surfaces. Both eyes are examined in sections which link to specific body zones. Colour and texture of the iris indicates the patient's health status and personality type which may predispose them to illness. Various flecks and marks on the eye indicate physical and emotional problems. It may be found that both past and present upsets are equally evident.

What happens: The iridologist photographs and examines both eyes. He then refers the patient to an appropriate therapist – often a nutritionist or naturopath – for treatment. The patient returns periodically for check-ups which chart the progress. People also often use iridology to monitor orthodox treatment, or as a health check-up.

Kinesiology

Good for: Problems that seem to defy other therapies. Especially psoriasis, ME, candida, PMS, allergies and bronchitis.

What it is: A system of diagnosis and treatment based on muscle testing. Developed in Canada by allergist Dr Jimmy Scott, health kinesiology works on the principle that the body knows exactly what it needs – so ask it! Muscles are linked to specific organs via meridians, or energy channels. They may also hold deep-seated emotional trauma which underlies illness. Muscle testing 'questions' the body, without involving the conscious mind.

What happens: You hold out each arm in turn, while the kinesologist asks health-related questions and applies light, tapping pressures. If the answer is 'yes', the arm stays still. If 'no', the muscle weakens and the arm drops. As well as diagnosing, tapping can also rid the body of intolerances and allergies.

Other energizing and clearing techniques may involve crystals, magnets, essential oils and homeopathic remedies, each of which are simply held against the body during treatment.

Pure plant power

Aromatherapy

Good for: An excellent stress-buster that helps counteract anxiety, insomnia, PMS and depression. Aromatherapy oils can be blended to control and rebalance skin problems, ease muscle strain, circulation and respiratory problems and to strengthen the immune system. They also make excellent natural first-aiders.

What it is: A treatment that combines massage with essential plant oils. Clinical studies constantly confirm that specific essential plant oils have a potent physiological and psychological effect. They soothe and relax, stimulate and help dispel depression. They also regulate body functions and some have potent antibiotic, antibacterial, antifungal and antiseptic actions. On-going studies at the University of Western Australia have already found that tea tree oil is an antiviral and antimicrobial agent powerful enough to kill the multi-resistant staphylococcus Aureus (MRSA), a rampant hospital bacteria that causes life-threatening wound infections. In time, it may also prove useful in anti-HIV spermicidals.

When inhaled, essential oils communicate with a part of the brain known as the limbic system, the pre-frontal brain on which our ancient ancestors depended for their survival before they developed the more sophisticated cerebral cortex, the part of the brain on which we now rely to interpret visual and oral information.

The limbic system is the emotional control centre of the brain. It is responsible for regulating appetite, sex drive and our stress response. The link between smell, emotion and memory is responsible for the psychotherapeutic power of aromatherapy. Odours are especially potent because they operate on a subliminal level and have direct access to the emotional centres of the brain without interference from rational thought processes. It is almost as if every memory has a fragrant tag attached to it, so that reintroducing a smell will not only spur vivid recollection of past events but will also reproduce the emotions aroused at the time of those events.

An essential oil can delight with its aroma, and with repeated use, can come to be associated with a receptive, enhanced but relaxed state of mind.

But essential oils do not simply work through association. Using EEGs to monitor electrical brain wave patterns in individuals when exposed to certain odours, we now know that some essential oils are relaxing, others reviving. This action on the autonomic nervous system results in physiological changes such as deeper respiration, slower heart rate and relaxed muscle tone. An odour can produce a physiological change as well as a psychological change.

In addition to their huge psychological impact, essential oils have a wide range of skin benefits. They can be antiseptic, antibiotic, antiviral and antifungal in action. They also have the ability to balance the production of sebum, making them useful for the variety of skin problems that result from too much or too little sebum.

Women are particularly susceptible to aromatherapy, possibly because of their acute and subtle sense of smell. Valerie Ann Worwood suggests not only do we have preferences according to our personality type, we can also inhale or massage ourselves with essential oils to counteract negative aspects of our psyche.

What happens: Aromatherapists use around 300 oils blended according to the conditions they treat. An aromatherapy massage is frankly, holistic bliss. A full body session may also include the face and feet, often incorporates pressure point manipulation (see below) and may last up to two hours. The ideal time for a treatment is at the end of the day, so that you can thoroughly relax afterwards. Part of aromatherapy's broad appeal is that you can blend

your own essential oils at home. From a therapeutic viewpoint, this is always more successful than using 'beauty' products with so-called aromatherapy ingredients. Many mass market firms use nature-identical fragrance molecules that smell good, but are rarely as effective as the real thing.

Aromatherapy any time

Essential oils can have a powerful effect and should be treated with respect. Never use them neat on your skin – some can cause irritation and some can burn. Instead, dilute them with a vegetable carrier oil, like jojoba, or sweet almond. Or use them in an oil burner as a therapeutic room fragrancer. Some oils should be avoided if you are pregnant. The best advice you'll get is from a qualified aromatherapist who will be able to suggest which are the best oils for you.

Many oils have shared benefits. Choosing one needn't be complicated though: try smelling them. The oil with the scent you like most is likely to have the most beneficial effect.

Here are some of the most popular essential oils, with suggested uses. Use all blends within 24 hours, and don't leave Aroma Jars burning for more than ten minutes at any one time.

Bergamot eases the stresses of the day and is thought to reduce worry and anxious feelings.

Sunshine massage: Add two drops of bergamot, one drop of lemon and 20 drops of pre-diluted neroli to 10mls of carrier oil. Blend well. Massage with light stimulating strokes in an upward direction.

Good start room fragrance: *Add four drops of bergamot to the dish of an Aroma Jar (or other oil burner) pre-filled with water – an excellent way to give work a kick-start in the morning.*

Camomile *is believed to soothe frayed nerves and take the heat out of any situation.*

Sweet dreams room fragrance: *Add four-five drops of camomile to the dish of an Aroma Jar pre-filled with water. As the vapours suffuse the room, you will feel yourself relaxing. This is especially good when putting over-tired children to bed.*

Comforting compress: *Add two drops each of camomile and lavender to a small bowl of warm water and blend well. Wet a clean flannel, squeeze out excess water, then apply to any area that feels over-heated. Avoid contact with the eyes.*

Eucalyptus *is great for clearing the head and reviving the body.*

Mental block: *Add three drops of eucalyptus on a handkerchief and inhale when you feel fuzzy-headed. Avoid direct skin contact with neat oil.*

Deep breath sauna formula: *Add four-five drops to a bucket of water and mix well before pouring over coals.*

Geranium *is considered one of life's great balancers, restoring a sense of harmony and equilibrium.*

Comfort massage: *Add two drops each of geranium and camomile and 20 drops of pre-diluted rose oil to 10mls carrier oil. Blend well. Especially good for dry, mature skins.*

Jasmine *is believed to relieve anxiety and uplift the spirit with its warm exotic odour.*

Sensuous massage: *Add 20 drops each of pre-diluted jasmine and rose and one drop of sandalwood to 10mls carrier oil. Blend well for a sensuous and seductive massage.*

Lavender *is another natural balancer, said to soothe the skin, calm body and mind and promote relaxation.*

Sleepy head: *Add two drops of lavender to a cotton wool ball and place inside your pillowcase.*

Skin balancer: *Add two drops of lavender and one drop of sandalwood to 10mls carrier oil. Blend well. Smooth onto skin to help balance skin's oil levels.*

Lemon *enhances concentration so it's a*

perfect pick-me-up for the mid-afternoon.

Lemon face sauna: *Blend one drop each of lemon, lavender and rosemary in a large bowl and add boiling water. Cover your head with a towel and, keeping eyes closed, steam your face gently. This helps balance a greasy skin.*

Fear of flying: *Add three drops of lavender and one drop of lemon to 300mls (½ pint) of cold water and blend well. Saturate cotton wool pads in the mixture, squeeze out excess liquid and pack in a plastic bag to use as refreshing and calming face wipes during your flight. Avoid contact with the eyes.*

Neroli, from the blossom of the bitter orange tree, is believed to calm nerves and boost self-confidence.

Supple skin mix: *Add 20 drops of pre-diluted neroli and two drops of lavender to 10mls of wheatgerm oil. Blend well. Apply with even upward strokes to the skin to keep it moisturized and supple.*

Light thoughts oil: *Add a few drops of neroli to 5mls of carrier oil. Blend well. Massage into the forehead and temples to promote relaxation. Avoid contact with the eyes.*

Peppermint helps you stay alert and focused, but it's not recommended for sensitive skin.

Cooling bath: *Add two drops each of peppermint and lavender to 10mls of carrier oil and blend well. Add it to the bath and enjoy the strangely stimulating effect.*

Exhaustion fumes: *Add six drops of peppermint and four drops of rosemary to 120mls (¼ pint) of pure still spring water in a misting bottle. Shake well and spray two or three times, inhaling deeply with eyes closed. Kept in the car, this is an ideal refresher for long journeys. (Don't use it all at once though!)*

Rose is believed to soften and cleanse the skin, and gently soothe emotions and worries.

Rose night-time facial: *Add 20 drops of pre-diluted rose to 10mls of carrier oil and blend well. Massage gently into the skin after cleansing for a night-time treat.*

Indian new year bath: *Add two drops of sandalwood and 20 drops of pre-diluted rose to 10mls of carrier oil. Blend well for a luxurious bath oil.*

Rosemary is the ultimate pick-me-up as it helps to fight off fatigue, stimulates the mind and also successfully revives the body.

Study stimulus: *Add two drops each of rosemary and lemon to the dish of an Aroma Jar, pre-filled with water, for a mental boost while studying.*

Foot fixer blend: *Add one drop each of rosemary, peppermint and geranium to a warm foot bath and blend well. Add one teaspoon of bicarbonate of soda. Soak feet for ten minutes.*

Sandalwood *stimulates the imagination and inspires new ideas and activities.*

Musky massage blend: *Add two drops each of sandalwood and lavender to 10mls of carrier oil. Then blend well for a deeply relaxing and sensual massage oil.*

Quiet place room fragrance: *Add two drops each of lemon and sandalwood to the dish of an Aroma Jar that has been pre-filled with water. The fragrance will help reduce anxiety and clear a spinning head.*

Ylang Ylang's *exotic floral smell has an instant soothing and relaxing effect. It also enjoys a reputation as an aphrodisiac.*

Oasis bath blend: *Add 20 drops of pre-diluted rose, and one drop each of ylang ylang and lavender to 10mls of carrier oil. Blend well for a luxurious, relaxing bath oil.*

Essential oil

extracted from

bergamot eases the

stresses of the day.

Herbalism

Good for: General first aid. Headaches and migraine. Arthritis and rheumatism. Skin, digestive and hormonal problems.

What it is: Plants were man's first medicine. Excavations indicate that neolithic societies prized certain plants and flowers for their sacred and healing associations. Many of today's modern drugs have their origins in traditional plant medicine. The most famous example is digitalis, or the foxglove, whose potential was first recognized by an 18th-century doctor, when he discovered that heart patients he thought would die got better after the village wise woman began dosing them with the plant. A synthesized form, Digoxin, is a key ingredient of modern heart drugs. Herbalists use the whole plant to treat illness – not extracts. If so-called 'active ingredients' are isolated, they may have side-effects that other compounds in the plant would buffer against.

Similarly, rather than treat isolated symptoms, herbalism holistically addresses the patient's physical, mental and emotional state. Getting down to underlying causes of illness is the surest way of restoring homeostasis – or total healthy balance. (See also Ayurveda and traditional Chinese medicine.)

What happens: The 1968 Medicines Act allows qualified medical herbalists to prescribe medications, which they make up for patients after a full consultation. You can also buy herbal creams, ointments, tinctures, teas and capsules at health stores and chemists. Herbal specialists sell loose, dried herbs that you can make into various therapeutic drinks. A decoction is made from dried herbs simmered for 20 minutes, strained, then sipped while the liquid is still hot. To make an infusion, use a dessertspoon of herb per cup of boiling water, leave to steep for ten minutes in a teapot, then drink hot or cold. A tincture is made by steeping herbs in a 25 per cent mixture of alcohol (like vodka) and water, leaving it for two weeks, then pressing and straining. The mixture, which keeps for up to two years, can be taken as drops, either neat or diluted in water.

You can also use herbs in poultices, compresses and as inhalants and mouthwashes. But treat with caution – herbs can be potent. Never exceed recommended doses and if you are pregnant or have a serious medical condition, check with your doctor or herbalist before taking herbal remedies or supplements.

A herbal first-aid kit

Herb	Good for	How to use
Feverfew (Tanacetum parthenium)	headaches, migraine	To prevent migraine, eat a leaf a day. While symptoms last, take 5-10 drops of tincture every 30 minutes.
Garlic (Allium sativum)	colds, flu	Eat up to six fresh cloves daily while symptoms are acute, or take capsules. Eat parsley to neutralize odour.
Purple coneflower (Echinacea spp)	sore throats	Gargle with 10ml tincture in a glass of warm water, then swallow the gargle.
Eyebright (Euphrasis officinalis)	conjunctivitis, red or puffy eyes	Soak a pad in an infusion and rest on closed lids. Bathe eyes in eyewash of 5-10 drops tincture in water.
Ground ivy (Glechoma hederacea)	hay fever, allergic rhinitis	Take as an infusion or tincture.
Lady's mantle (Alchemilla vulgaris)	PMT, tenderness and bloating	Take as a tincture or infusion. Avoid during pregnancy.
Linden (Tilia europaea)	stress, high blood pressure	Sip as an infusion of tisane. Take up to 10ml tincture daily.

Homeopathy

Good for: General first aid, allergies, chronic illness, digestive problems, emotional and menstrual problems.

What it is: A system using plant, mineral and animal substances to treat illness on a 'hair of the dog' basis. Whereas allopathic or conventional medicine counteracts symptoms, homeopathy delivers diluted amounts of natural agents that in normal doses, would produce a similar effect to the infection or disease. This shocks our own 'vital force' into healing mode. The idea of treating like with like dates back to Hippocrates. The 16th-century physician Paracelsus also believed that each disease held the key to its cure. Homeopathy was founded in the 18th century after a German doctor Samuel Hahnemann found that giving chinchona bark (quinine) to healthy subjects produced symptoms of malaria. When given to sufferers, it cured the fever. He then developed a pharmacy of substances following the same principles.

What happens: Hahnemann believed that a person's body type and personality influenced their reaction to disease and both are taken into account when prescribing homeopathic cures. Remedies come in tablet, powder, granules, cream or drop formulas and are available from health stores and pharmacies. In normal doses, substances like arsenic and belladonna can kill. Yet in minute dilutions, they have non-toxic healing powers. Homeopathic remedies are diluted thousands of times until only traces of their molecules are left. A decimal dilution of 6x equals one part in a million; and a centesimal dilution of 12x is said to be like a pinch of salt in the Atlantic Ocean. The weaker the solution, the more effective the cure. This potency relies on the theory that a substance can leave its 'memory' imprinted on the medium that dilutes it. Popular remedies include arnica for shocks and bruises; rhus tox for sprains and strains; calendula for skin problems, and gelsemium for influenza.

Flower essence remedies

Good for: Treating the emotions underlying physical conditions. Widely used for stress, anger, grief, lack of confidence and low self-esteem.

What it is: Flower remedies were first devised in the 1930s by British pathologist and bacteriologist Dr Edward Bach. Intuition told him that specific flower essences could balance mood and personality traits, allaying the negative, encouraging the positive and stimulating resistance to stress and disease. Bach often saw human characteristics in plants. Impatiens (Busy Lizzie) for example, is said to offset impatience and irritability. Heather – a plant that tolerates few others in its vicinity – is taken to counteract self-centredness. Fear, indecision, apathy, despair, self-loathing and even loneliness all have their flower remedies.

Bach initially captured the essence of 38 flowers by bottling the dew on their leaves and petals. Later he used spring water in which petals floated for three hours in full sunlight. He believed that the plant transferred its vibrational qualities to the water by means of molecular imprinting. The energized water was then strained and brandy added as a preservative.

What happens: Take the essences as needed, either dropped onto the tongue, rubbed onto the forehead, lips, wrists, soles and palms or added to your bathwater, moisturizer or body lotion. Bach's most famous tincture, Rescue Remedy, has become something of a cult cure-all. A blend of rock rose, impatiens, clematis, star of Bethlehem and cherry plum, it claims to soothe you after shock and calm panic or ease grief and depression. In cream form it can also soothe skin irritation and inflammation.

Since Bach's day, many other systems have flourished. In the 1970s, an American Richard Kratz bottled 70 Californian flower essences and there are now ranges from all over the world. Australian bush essences include the whimsical Billy Goat Plum for low self-esteem and Kangaroo Paw for gaucheness. Hawaiian essences are more 'new agey' and include panini-awa'awa for mending holes in your aura and naupaka-kahakai to raise your spiritual profile.

One of the most progressive ways of using flower essences is to enhance weight control. In London, husband and wife team Nicola and Maurice Griffin combine nutritional and Bach flower therapy to alleviate weight, digestion and food allergy problems. They believe that digestive disturbances often result from negative childhood influences which then become compounded by adult stress. Irritable bowel syndrome, Crohns disease, bulimia and anorexia nervosa are all examples. Useful flower essences like crab apple and agrimony ease self-loathing, compulsion and addiction. Cherry plum works on lack of control and larch restores confidence. Combined with a new nutritional blueprint, their effects can be liberating.

mind body soul

'The soul is the voice of the body's interests.'
George Santayana, 1905

Food for the soul: a celebration of self-esteem

Ritual, symbol and ceremony are enduring elements of humankind's history. You would probably be surprised at the degree to which you ritualize your daily behaviour: how you get up, how you prepare yourself for the day, how you eat, how you behave in your relationships, even the tiniest things, the special way you fold your laundry, for instance. As an expression of force of habit, ritual can be a great source of comfort. It can also be a way to celebrate a transition or an event, or, on an altogether grander scale, an ordered spiritual experience. Ritual and ceremony are valuable tools in the quest for wellbeing as they can help bridge the gap between body and soul.

With their closeness to nature, women in particular have an instinctive feel for the symbolic. One great difficulty for women is being able to focus on their own needs without feeling selfish. They need to feel that the idea of nurturing themselves – to feed their souls – is an act of self-respect. And for that, they need to look within.

That was always the purpose of prayer. As a symbolic ritual for communicating with a 'higher power', it was a simple way to look inside for the purposes of relaxation and nurturing. Even now, prayer is a highly personal ritual. You can do it alone or communally, out loud or in silence. You can follow the liturgies you learned in youth or make up your own prayers. Some women sing and dance,

others paint or perform to feel at one with their world.

Another way to foster this holistic spirit is to learn the art of being: just relaxing, feeling at peace with yourself. Much of this book has been devoted to just that, but the point bears making over and over.

Being is most often associated with meditation, whose techniques can calm and centre us. But meditation is still an act of doing. Being is about existing in a non-doing state, listening for guidance from the soul, breathing, scanning the body's subtle ebb and flow for information. People who practise yoga often say it's the state of mind they're in after a session. And once you've experienced it, it becomes a necessary antidote to a full day of activity. The big problem is that the more you do, the harder it is to simply be.

It's too easy for mothers to feel they're wasting time, not being productive. In many cases, the only time a woman allows herself the time to be still is on holiday or when she is ill. It is easier to rush to return phone calls instead of really talking to a friend, to start another load of laundry rather than sinking down for a rest in a sun-filled garden. Our society, with its stress-related conditions, makes a stark contrast with cultures that aren't based on productivity and materialism, where women can harmonize work, play and family obligations.

The new popularity of massage therapy and healing has given many overworked Western women a chance to recognize and let go of their stress. Though learning to be at peace is not necessarily everyone's ideal way of relaxing, if you are lucky enough to acquire a technique which harmonizes mind and body, you can find the state of calm that prevails in places of worship such as an old church, a Buddhist temple or a retreat centre.

relax

The challenge is particularly acute for mothers. It feels easier to keep going, to do the dishes instead of stopping and checking in with yourself.

harmony

Our society, with its stress-related conditions, makes a stark contrast with cultures that aren't based on productivity and materialism, where women can harmonize work, play and family obligations.

sacred

The knack of creating a sacred space is to introduce one small area of satisfaction into your life that makes you proud and happy.

celebrate

We all become pretty good at ceremonies, as children playing make-believe or hosting birthday parties, as adults with our weddings, baptisms and funerals.

health

Fundamental to shamanism is spiritual health and the individual's ability to appreciate their place within the universe, as if we are a microcosmic reflection of the greater whole.

A sacred space in the home

Think of it as making a sacred space for yourself. The knack of creating a sacred space is to introduce one small area of satisfaction into your life that makes you proud and happy. It takes courage and commitment to create such a change, especially when society so often seems to insist that you don't. Make a start by asking yourself these simple questions:

What do I truly enjoy?

How can I find a way to enjoy my body?

What do I like working on in a creative way?

How and where can I find the time to enjoy something different?

Your sacred place represents the spiritual heart of the home. It can be any room or corner of a room. The most popular places are in and around a fireplace, study or bedroom. Clear your space of clutter, redecorate it, add pictures of family and favourite friends, items that have some personal significance for you, objects from nature such as crystals, stones, wood, flowers. You can also make space for yourself in other, simpler ways, with a couple of provisos. Avoid shopping, alcohol, looking in the mirror, body wraps, leg waxing and any competition or confrontation. And ask family or flatmates to leave you the space for a day, or just an evening if a day is asking too much.

Making space in the home

 Spend a whole day in bed, reading, talking with friends on the phone, watching television, eating favourite foods such as chocolates or ice cream, just thinking.

 Arrange for someone to come over and give you a massage, followed by a time to sleep or rest with no interruptions (no calls, no kids).

 Paint. Create something with paints or crayons, oils, acrylics, pencils, a large painting block and a full day to yourself. Don't fret about technique or style.

 Read. Spend unlimited time reading something for enjoyment. Go to the library or browse through a bookshop.

 Listen to music. Relax and listen to your favourite tapes or CDs with no interruptions.

 Bathe. Place lots of candles around the bathroom, use some essential oils in the bath and relax in silence.

 Write a diary, a poem, a story, a song, without editing or expectation.

A sacred space in nature

**The natural world refreshes like nothing else. It can even suggest
solutions to your own problems by putting them in perspective.**

All over the world, there are thousands of places in nature that have been revered
for millennia as ceremonial or healing sites. Stonehenge, Avebury and Glastonbury
in the UK, Delphi in Greece, Ayers Rock in Australia, Table Mountain in Capetown
and Mount Shasta in California are just a few. But, with a little work, you can find
your own sacred space in nature. Elemental impulses find their elemental
complement in earth, wind and water.

Making space in nature

 Spend at least two days and one night living as closely as you dare with nature. Wake up with the sun, sleep with the dark, eat only when you are hungry. No television, no telephone, no distractions.

 Go to a park, woodland or natural place close by. Lie on the ground, listen to your heart and gradually feel the earth beneath you. As you relax, your perspective changes.

 Listen to water. Sit by the ocean or a river, or even out in the rain. It is the best treatment nature can offer for calming the emotions.

 Trees can be very comforting. Take off for an hour or two, find a tree, sit up in its branches if you can climb it or just lie with your back against the trunk.

 Stand at the edge of a cliff or high point on a hill or mountain. Feel the wind blowing around your body, washing away stress and strain. Enjoy the feeling of being up so high.

Ceremonies

Celebration is a primal human impulse that finds its expression in the ceremony. The big communal ceremonies of our culture are inescapable (think about the Oscars or the Olympic Games), but we all become pretty good at ceremonies, as children playing make-believe or hosting birthday parties, as adults with our weddings, baptisms and funerals. A different perspective on these ceremonies can make them enjoyable and soulful at the same time.

One family's ceremony for a new-born

A family on the West Coast of Scotland wanted to mark the birth of their first child. They based their ceremony on their Christian and Celtic origins but the idea behind the celebration can be adapted by anyone from any background.

'As the Celtic traditions were very connected with the powers of the moon, we felt the best time for a gathering would be the first day of the full moon following the birth. We invited family and close friends, and everyone was expected to bring a gift, and something to eat and drink. My girlfriend and sister helped organize everything because I was exhausted from feeding and caring for our new baby.

'It was midsummer so we felt it would be more powerful to have a celebration outside in our garden. To prepare a sacred place in the garden we chose our favourite tree. We placed a small bowl of water and a small bowl of salt around the tree, and lit three candles for the three cycles of the moon. The atmosphere was enhanced by my husband putting fairy lights around the tree. When everyone had arrived, we held hands around the tree, said the Lord's Prayer and sang a song to celebrate the arrival of our daughter. I asked for the guidance and protection of our baby and named her and her godparents. Then the godparents gave gifts and messages of goodwill for us and the baby, and our family and friends spoke in turn sending our child different gifts and visions for her future. My husband and the godfather planted a rowan tree in our daughter's name and buried the placenta and umbilical cord under it. The rowan has significant magical properties of protection, the placenta makes good fertilizer, and we had read that in ancient times women used to bury the afterbirth. Then we all had a dram of whiskey to celebrate and the party began.

'This was the first time that we as a family ever held a ceremony. It made an unforgettable event even more emotional and powerful.'

A mother and daughter celebrate first blood

This event is rarely celebrated in modern culture but first blood is an important time of transition for a girl. It is often the moment for a mother to talk to her daughter about birth control, different methods of coping with her period and her sexuality.

A divorced mother and her 13-year-old daughter had not been getting on since the dissolution of her marriage two years earlier. The idea of holding a party for her daughter's upcoming birthday was to allow them to hold an adult event together. Around that time, her daughter's first period arrived. Early one morning, her daughter came into her bedroom and, to her mother's surprise, wanted to share this sensitive moment.

'She agreed that it was special and she would love to hold a gathering of women friends and family to come together to celebrate her womanhood. We organized a party the following month, which was a great success. I bought her a ring with a garnet. My mother suggested it would be very good for her as a blood stone such as a garnet is a strong symbol. The party brought us closer together because as I learned that if I accepted and loved her for who she was, she found the ability to accept and love me too. We became friends.'

A celebration of menopause

Victoria, a single woman in her late forties, had reached that point in her life when she was exhausted – consumed by career with no steady relationship. At a lunch date with a colleague, she broached the idea of getting away for a weekend to find space in their lives to let go of the past and bring in a new vision for their future.

'We booked a weekend in a country-house about two hours from the city with six women friends. We took mementoes of our pasts: photographs, copies of marriage and divorce papers, a lock of each child's hair, a picture we'd painted when we were small, anything that represented a turning point in our lives.

'The first evening was settling in, getting out all the mementoes, telling stories about the past. The second day was organized in advance so that each woman spent the afternoon alone, exploring the emotions involved with each item, writing down feelings, or just letting them well up. By the time everyone gathered in the evening to discuss what they felt about how their life had been, a lot of emotion had accumulated. The atmosphere at dinner was difficult, but gradually everyone opened up: cried, talked, even shouted, about not being attractive to men any more, about the pressure of single motherhood, about disappointment.

'The following day was set up as a day to find new ways of coming to terms with this empty space. We all wrote down our grievances and disappointments and went alone into nature to make peace with ourselves. Some of us buried our stories, others built a small fire and burnt them, or spent time just walking or sitting by a tree, feeling the loss.

'That afternoon before going back, we arranged another weekend a month later to bring with us ideas and images of the things that we wanted to bring into our future. We collected them from magazines, books, photographs and paintings that inspired us. Did we want to travel more, paint, create a garden, write poetry, find a lover? Did we want to find a new avenue in our careers, move house, leave our families, learn a language, take a degree, get in touch with a spiritual power or healing gift?

'We spent the weekend looking and feeling much happier with ourselves, returning to the places where we had buried our past, sitting building our future, writing down a list of goals and dating it with a 12-month step programme. Then we spent the rest of the evening drinking champagne, eating our favourite foods, dancing and celebrating. The next time we will gather is in 12 months to celebrate our plans.'

Shamanism

One visible illustration of our renewed appreciation of the role of ritual and ceremony in our lives is curiosity about the role of the shaman. It is a thread that runs through all times, all cultures. Traditionally, a shaman has been a wise man or woman, who, through contact with the spirit world, is responsible for the health of the community and its environment. Ecology is integral – the universe is the shaman's teacher and metaphors found in nature are his guides. Fundamental to shamanism is spiritual health and the individual's ability to appreciate their place within the universe, as if we are a microcosmic reflection of the greater whole.

According to the historian Ward Rutherford, shamanic tradition stretches back 20,000 years. There is evidence of shamanism as early as Neolithic times in Scandinavia and in Indo-European cultures before the great migrations. Mongolian, Siberian, Tibetan, Korean, Eskimo, North and South American, African, Polynesian and Antipodean cultures all have their shamanic traditions. In Britain, the Celtic and Druidic traditions embrace shamanism.

So what makes a shaman? The word comes from saman, from the Tungas people of Siberia and may have derived from the Sanskrit sramana, meaning an ascetic who becomes excited or moved. One definition of a shaman is 'wounded healer'. Shamans have invariably undergone some personal crisis, either physical or psychological, leading to a psychic death and rebirth, which has changed their entire perception. The contemporary American shaman Denise Linn was actually shot by a rogue sniper and underwent a near-death experience; Nicki Scully, another American shaman, was struck with leukaemia. Initiation can also happen through dreams and visions, or insights. Shamanic rituals such as those outlined overleaf develop spiritual awareness and intuition.

The medicine wheel

This teaches us how to integrate with and honour our environment. The four compass directions also represent the four kingdoms of animal, plant, mineral and human; the four elements of earth, air, fire and water; and the four human aspects of body, mind, emotion and spirit.

Shape shifting

'Becoming' the other person, plant or animal is a technique of psychic projection in order to appreciate and understand their condition.

Shamanic journeying

Shamanic journeying is a form of meditation or guided visualization, which throws light on a situation from a different perspective, or Otherworld. In this Otherworld, you may also meet your spirit guide or power animal, such as the eagle, owl, bear or dear. Power animals act as totems and have attributes of the shaman's personality and 'energy' and guide his or her healing work. Nicki Scully, for example, calls upon mythical Egyptian animals, like the lion goddess Sekhmet. Shamans also derive their ritual names from their animals – like the American feminist shaman, Starhawk.

The sweat lodge ceremony

The sauna-like atmosphere of this ceremony represents physical trial and ritual purification. A cathartic, often uncomfortable experience, it prepares you for journeying and heightens perception.

Trance dancing and drumming

Central to insight, these are the traditional vehicles that induce a shift in consciousness. At first slower than a heartbeat, then increasingly faster, the drum is the 'horse' whose rhythm the shaman rides on his visionary journey. 'Urban' shaman Gabrielle Roth, who runs workshops in the US and UK, teaches ecstatic trance-dancing in five sequential rhythms – flowing, staccato, chaos, lyrical and stillness – each representing stages of the shamanic journey. UK shaman Jill Purce teaches 'overtone' chanting and freestyle voicework as yet another route to ecstasy.

As well as divination through runes and tarot, shamanic healing often embraces other therapies, like Reiki, crystal healing and aromatherapy. Kahuna bodywork is a massage with its roots in Hawaiian shamanism. Said to work on a vibrational level that boosts cellular energy, the rhythmic and repetitive movements affect both the physical and etheric body or aura – the electromagnetic field that surrounds us. The ultimate aim is to help you love your body whatever its shape and raise your self-esteem, so you're better able to live in harmony with creation as a

whole. Denise Linn's own transcadence massage is based on the transformational power of drumming. The body is massaged by a series of percussive hand rhythms that relax, energize and inspire physical and emotional changes.

Shamanism is a popular vehicle for personal development. Methods vary, but the majority of shamans in both the US and UK follow North and South American Indian traditions and rituals. Jungian psychotherapists show an increasing interest in shamanism and the use of its metaphors in personal problem-solving and everyday situations. Certainly, Carl Jung's theories on the collective unconscious and synchronicity (meaningful coincidence) fit perfectly with shamanic practise. The first analyst to use

shamanic technique in therapy was the late, controversial RD Laing. His pupil Anthony Lunt now carries on his work.

Shamans may also adapt psychotherapeutic techniques like gestalt and mirror work. But a word of caution – check out a shaman's qualifications. Remember that you are dealing with the mind and emotions and whereas some people will find this liberating, to others it can be confrontational, scary stuff. An unprofessional approach without a sound basis can leave you highly emotionally and psychologically vulnerable. If you have suffered psychiatric illness or are undergoing counselling or analysis, it's wise to inform your doctor or therapist before you embark on a course of shamanic healing.

Going on a shamanic journey

Use this visualization technique to help you contact your spirit guides and develop insight into a problem.

- Sit or lie in a quiet room. Close your eyes and take ten deep, slow breaths.
- Imagine you are walking through a forest. Concentrate on the sights and sounds around you.
- You come to a door set in a wall. Turn the handle and step through.
- Be aware of all you see and meet on the other side.
- To return from the journey, focus on the room in which you are lying, and breathe deeply again.

Feng shui: wellbeing in your environment

You can rearrange your environment so that it benefits you spiritually and physically. That is the central principle of feng shui, an ancient Chinese art that aims to find out what you need to be more successful in life and then adjusts the atmosphere of your home and workplace to help you achieve your goals. This 'adjustment' happens by manipulating the flow of *chi* energy through a room or building, in the same way that acupuncture or shiatsu does with the body. In fact, feng shui has been called 'space acupuncture'. As your own *chi* energy extends between 10 cm and 1 m (4 and 39 in) beyond your skin, it is easily influenced by the *chi* energy of your surroundings. Harmonize your surroundings and you will inspire harmony in your body and soul.

Each building has its own *chi* energy. Sitting on your own in a large cathedral will encourage particular thoughts and emotions as your *chi* energy mixes with the building's. You will likely think about the big issues in your life. You will feel clearer, more spiritual. But meet someone in a small, crowded cafe and your *chi* energy will mix with the café's more active, intimate and cosy energy. You will feel more practical, social and oriented to issues that are close to you.

Over the thousands of years that feng shui has evolved and migrated into other parts of Asia, various styles have developed. The style we will detail here is known as the compass method because it is based on the influence of the sun, the planets and the earth's magnetic field on *chi* energy. Though the *chi* energy of a building is determined by many factors, the sun generally has the greatest impact on the atmosphere in each part of the building.

Feng shui divides a building into eight wedges starting from the centre. Each area will have a particular flow of *chi* energy that can influence your own, and therefore your thoughts and ideas, in a particular way.

Improving your feng shui

The **east** part of your home is influenced by the rising sun – the beginning of the day – and is therefore associated with starting new projects, being ambitious and becoming active.

The **south-east** area is exposed to the sun as it rises through the morning sky. This *chi* energy helps you feel positive, more communicative and creative.

The **south** is warmed by the sun when it is at its highest position. This fiery *chi* energy helps you feel more emotional, expressive and passionate.

The **south-west** segment of your home receives direct sunlight as the sun descends in the afternoon. This more settled energy will encourage you to be more practical and thoughtful, and also to consolidate what you already have.

The **west side** of your home will face the sunset – the end of the day – and is therefore linked to completing projects, feelings of contentment and also to romance and financial success.

The **north-west** area is influenced by the evening haze which is associated with looking back on the day. This is helpful for feeling more in control of your life and developing a sense of wisdom.

The **north** faces the equivalent of the middle of the night. This, the quietest direction, helps generate feelings of deep inner peace, spirituality and objectivity.

The **north-east** section is subject to a sharper, more penetrating chi energy, similar to the cold north-eastern winds. It can help you feel more motivated, competitive and hard-working.

Spend more time in one of these parts of your home and your own *chi* energy will receive a greater charge of the corresponding energy from the environment. And if you work or sleep so that the top of your head points in the direction that has chi energy that would most help you, you may slowly bring those qualities into your life.

There are other improvements anyone can make to a home without any specialist knowledge. These are designed to keep *chi* energy healthy and flowing harmoniously through your home.

Grow a variety of indoor plants at home. These add more living chi energy, help moderate fast-flowing energy and stimulate areas where the energy is stagnant. Place plants with pointed leaves – a yucca, for example – in corners to stimulate the flow of chi energy. Floppy or bushy plants with rounded leaves are better for easing the flow of energy around a sharp protruding corner or in a long corridor.

Try to fill your home with natural fibres and materials: cotton, linen, wool, silk, wood, ceramics, stone and metal. Synthetic materials tend to block the flow of *chi* energy. Synthetic clothing, bed linen and carpets can build up their own charge of static electricity that will adversely affect your *chi* energy, manifesting as tiredness or tension.

Within reason, keep your home as clean and tidy as possible, which keeps *chi* energy fresh and healthy and flowing smoothly. Clutter, dirt and dust increase the risk of stagnant energy, and you may find yourself feeling depressed and frustrated. Dampness or mildew in your bathroom will make *chi* energy more heavy and stagnant. Try to keep it as dry as possible.

Colours influence *chi* energy because each colour radiates its own frequency which affects your thoughts and emotions. One of the most effective ways to introduce

colour into a room is with fresh flowers or a flowering plant. Red flowers can help you feel more romantic and stylish, purple can add more passion to your *chi* energy, yellow will help you feel more powerful, and blue considerably more serene.

Choosing a feng shui consultant

As there is no formal training or apprenticeship in feng shui, many practitioners will have studied and qualified in a related subject such as traditional Oriental medicine, acupuncture or shiatsu. They may also be registered with the Feng Shui Society whose members agree to follow a code of ethics and have insurance.

You should ask questions about a consultant's training, length of practice, what style is used, whether the fee includes a written report and drawings, whether there are any extra charges for travel, if the feng shui astrology and on-going advice are included, and if you can talk to other clients.

wellbeing and the soul

Creation in the natural world is a constantly evolving spiral of birth, growth, parenting, letting go, death and regeneration. Within their own bodies and psyches, women experience some of the power of these creative forces. From infancy to elderhood, each chapter of a woman's life is distinguished by unique challenges and profound changes in personality which inevitably lead her to a deeper connection with her inner resources and the cycles of nature. This is the soul of wellbeing.

The mysteries of female biology dominated early human religions and art. Women were literate in the language of herbs and healing, and the oral traditions of the hearth. Mothers were responsible for the silent, mysterious education of the home, and their wisdom was openly revered for at least 15,000 years of Europe's pre-history, when there existed a highly developed culture based not on weapons or fear, but on reverence for the Great Goddess, or the Great Mother, a symbol of humankind's relationship with nature. The myth of the Goddess was based on her creative power expressed through the massive volumes of her body, the hills, rivers and mountains that surrounded humanity. She represented all aspects of human nature. So Goddess-oriented religions were organic and holistic. Daily tasks held cosmic meaning, like the Navajo Indian women weaving blankets and carpets in emulation of the Great Spiderwoman, the original weaver of the Universe.

The many texts and books on the Goddess carry the same messages: the Great Mother was connected with all of life and the body; the mind and spirit of all women were interwoven as a whole that represented Creation. Women are increasingly rediscovering that ancient interaction between themselves and the forces of the natural world. If you accept Carl Jung's theories at face value, you can see how this suggests that the female collective unconciousness must be a place of infinite richness and variety.

In fact, in talking to women from different generations and cultural backgrounds, one of the most striking similarities is the rich inner life that women share. Modern women with no religious affiliations speak about their life's journey in spiritual terms – the ecstasy of sexual intimacy, the miracle of childbirth, the unconditional love of parenting, the courage and insights which they discover in their most difficult times and the solace that they find in the stillness of nature. These instinctive responses are a wonderful foundation for a healthy sense of wellbeing because they remain grounded in the power of the body. So, through healing and nurturing their physical selves, helped by alternative methods of holistic healthcare, women can strengthen their self-esteem and find new harmony in their lives.

The cycles

Menstruation: a new perspective for women

Women directly experience the cyclical ebb and flow of life, not just in a nightly and daily rhythm but also in moon cycles. The four dramatic changes in the cycle of the moon – quarter phase, wax, full, wane – produce a corresponding effect on a woman's menstrual cycles. Her energy will wax, peak, then wane again, affecting her physically, sexually and spiritually. By being sensitive to her cycles and taking care to understand them, a woman can enhance her self-confidence and self-awareness.

Nothing in her life reminds a woman of the connection between body, mind and emotions like her period, as the physical discomforts of pre-menstrual syndrome such as bloating or sore breasts spill over into depression, irritability or insomnia, to name just three familiar symptoms. Medical researchers believe pre-menstrual tension is caused by a hormonal imbalance and women who are particularly prone to PMT either have too much oestrogen or too little progesterone. As modern society turns to a more holistic approach to healthcare, therapists such as naturopaths and nutritionists are now finding that when PMT sufferers are given high doses of vitamin B complexes, zinc, selenium, and evening primrose oil and asked to change their diet, many of them note a lessening of their physical and psychological symptoms.

spiritual

Modern women with no religious affiliations speak about their life's journey in spiritual terms - the ecstasy of sexual intimacy, the miracle of childbirth, the unconditional love of parenting, and the solace that they find in the stillness of nature.

birth

In many tribal societies, it is said that a man proves himself in the hunt or in battle, but a woman proves herself in birthing. Birth and motherhood offer an unparalleled opportunity for growth and the experience of love.

destiny

It is the destiny of mothers and daughters to give birth to each other, over and over. There is an umbilical link between puberty and menopause, the two great transitional phases in a woman's life.

letting go

The frailties that we suffer as we approach death are simply part of the process of letting go. Our bodies are helping us to relinquish life in its physical form.

In our society, there is a tendency for women to go about their business, disregarding entirely cyclical changes of mood or suppressing them by an effort of will. Certainly for the last century at least, women have been taught only to resent the discomfort and interference that their menstrual cycles have on their daily lives, instead of learning to understand them. But they can be viewed as a positive experience, because they may compel a woman to recognize a deeper layer of her own psychic life. Symptoms of physical and emotional disturbance can indicate a conflict between her conscious attitude and the demands of her own inner nature. If she recognizes such symptoms for what they are, she can take a step towards reconciling her outer and inner lives. Quiet time alone for a woman helps to establish a calming, private space (see page 200). Even when the pressures of the world are greater than the calming influence of this private space, the connection becomes stronger each time it is returned to, until eventually it can be entered at will. Such voluntary self-seclusion takes practice, but once a routine is set, a woman will find that the irritation and restlessness which ordinarily disturb her during her period will disappear. Instead of being pulled down and depleted, she can touch base with the deepest resources of her own feminine nature. This is what is meant by a new perspective.

In societies where the simple facts of nature are less controlled and civilized by personal ego and the pressures of living and working in an urban environment, women arrange their lives around the cycles of the moon, alternating a time of seclusion with work at home and in the community, with family and social life. Consider, for example, many Native American tribes, where a woman's menstrual time is spent alone in the menstrual lodge fasting and performing other purification rites. These are believed to be the equivalent of the initiation ceremonies that are practised by boys at puberty.

Before their initiations, boys spend time alone in the woods, devoting themselves to fasting, purging and the sweat bath. The ordeal is designed to bring the initiate into direct touch with deeper layers of his unconscious. The voice of his own true nature is released from his childishness and dependence on his parents.

Because a girl is believed to be already instinctively in touch with her true nature, her initiation is the pain and blood of her womb opening and releasing her first cycle. At this time she celebrates with her mother and grandmother to feel a connection with all women. She then goes to a lodge for menstrual women where she can be at peace and alone with herself.

As in those ancient tribal rituals, menarche – a girl's first period – can be an opportunity for mothers and daughters to confront some of the personal issues that surround womanhood. Girls usually discuss menstruation with their mothers and friends long before they get their first period and most say that they felt supported and empowered by their mothers the first time that they 'came on'. 'My Mum was great when I got my period,' says 15-year-old Sophie.

'I was really shy to tell her but we went for a long walk and talked about everything – sex, boys and contraception. She made me feel proud and quite grown up. I thought it was going to be much worse than it actually was. Now I get it regularly and I don't mind it really.'

Pregnancy

Sometimes painful, other times blissful, the integration of a woman's mind, body and soul is enhanced by pregnancy. Many women experience their pregnancies in a spiritual way. Others find the experience physically demanding and difficult. Pregnancy is the time to allow emotions to be felt and expressed with no inhibition.

In the early stages of pregnancy, the unborn child evolves from innocent form to personality within the safety of the womb. As the physiological, hormonal and emotional connection between them grows, the clash between the self of the woman and the child can cause many reactions in the early months, the most common being sickness, depression, tiredness, vivid dreaming, clumsiness and irrational moods. These are caused by hormonal changes in the body but they are also emotional and psychological reactions to the pregnancy. Body and soul are growing out of maidenhood into motherhood, letting the old life go, a painful but empowering process.

As the body acclimatizes to a new hormonal system, the pregnancy becomes a little easier. Morning sickness has disappeared (in most cases) by the fifth month. The mother-to-be is now radiant and healthy, at her most active: working, keeping fit, preparing the home for the arrival of the new child.

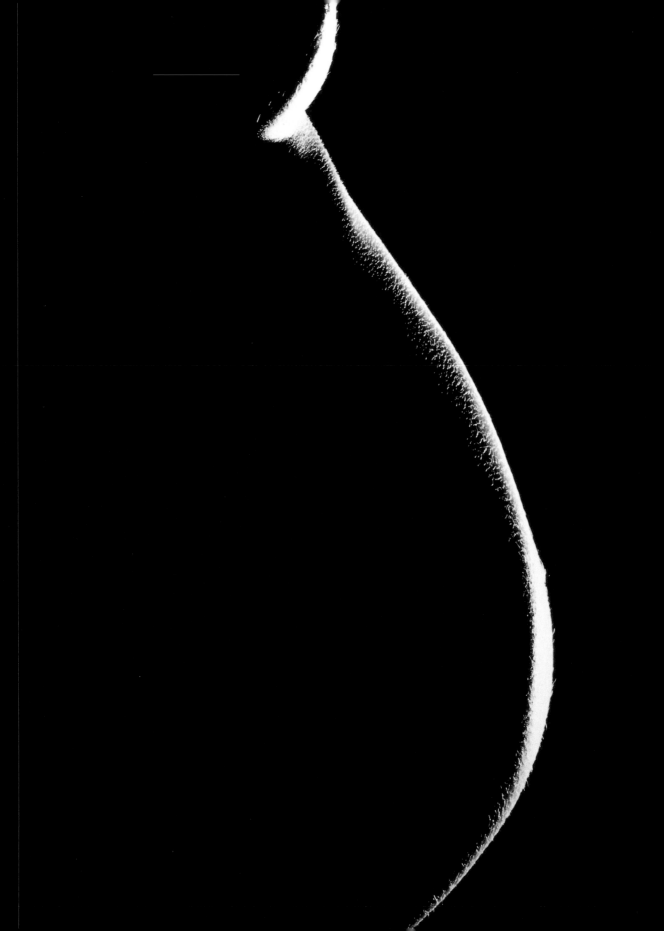

The soul of the baby remembers her past while in the womb and begins sensing the emotions and patterns of the mother and father, learning to respond to outside stimuli. The pregnant woman will notice periods of great stillness and times of tremendous energy and activity in her belly as the child responds to noise, light, music, movement, voices and people.

Non-verbal communication continues throughout the pregnancy as the physiological, hormonal and emotional connection between mother and child is fused. If the mother experiences any grief, sadness, or stress through overwork, a past miscarriage or still-born birth, family pressure and family death, the child will absorb these emotions and feelings. Some women are tortured by fears that the baby may be abnormal. It is not difficult for any pregnant woman to think back to something that occurred in the first weeks of pregnancy which might have harmed her baby: drugs, alcohol, a fall or accident. In addition, after a late miscarriage or still-birth, a woman is often waiting for the same thing to happen in her current pregnancy.

This is the time for a woman to get to know the child growing inside her. It is important to find sacred time for herself outside the needs of work and family; to withdraw from an active life, looking inward to nurture and enjoy her new sensitivity. Women often play music to their unborn child. Swimming, walking, dance, yoga and active birth classes are popular methods for preparing the body for birth. If a woman can establish a routine for claiming her own private space within the family or relationship at this stage, then she will find that the habit can last into the strenuous post-natal period. In the final stages of pregnancy, a mother-to-be may begin to become fearful about the birth, the pain and the ability to cope with motherhood. Sheila Kitzinger counsels:

'One way of counteracting this fear is to get together with other pregnant women to start exploring childbirth choices and weighing up the alternatives … a woman who feels that she is trapped inside her pregnant body may feel quite different once she starts exercise classes and learns how to breath and relax and prepare for birth.'

Now that the baby is fully formed, pressures in the back and cervix build up, causing considerable discomfort. Western women also suffer from the stereotypes of ideal body shapes and may feel fat or heavy and unhappy with their weight. Resistance to her changing personality may leave a woman feeling angry, irritable and depressed. If she can relax into her pregnancy, it becomes easier to enjoy the last few weeks. A healthy and communicative relationship with her partner and a doctor or midwife will also help her feel confident and secure about the birth.

Birth

It is important that a woman makes her choice about giving birth out of her instinct for what feels right for her: at home or in a hospital, in water, on her back or on all fours. Then she will be able to enter the experience of giving birth with the confidence and strength that all went well for her. One mother recalls her birth experience:

'I didn't realize I was in transition and felt I wanted to push. I was worried as this seemed far too early to push and I felt I was in the wrong position, so the midwife helped me turn from being on all fours to sitting up in a squat. I found that eye contact with my husband was important at this stage. When I felt panic during transition, my husband breathed with me to slow my breathing down. This immediately put me back in control of the powerful sensations in my body.'

If she feels safe, a first-time mother is able to surrender to the rhythms which overcome her as her cervix and womb open. She is able to trust her body and to cope with each mounting wave of pain which threatens to overwhelm her. The ability to surrender to and ride the wave has been compared to an act of

shamanism. 'Always awesome, it is not gentle or romantic, but like red hot fire ... both agony and ecstasy,' writes Janet Balaskas, founder of the Active Birth Movement.

Just before the baby's head emerges from the womb and travels through the channel to the vagina, the mother enters the final initiation. At that moment, she may feel as though she is going to die – or that she wants to die. The psyche often experiences a death for the gift of life. Once the head comes through, the pain stops and the baby is released from the womb. The movement of the placenta becomes sensual as it falls from the wall of the womb and follows the child into the world. 'Many women talk of sublime mystical transcendental states of orgasmic release that sometimes occur as a baby is born,' writes Janet Balaskas. Immediately after the birth, hormones released into the system create a surreal space and an unreal consciousness that give the mother a deep sense of euphoric delight.

The first step into motherhood

For most of womankind, motherhood is a mixed experience: on the one hand, the image of the 'radiant mother', on the other, the mundane realities of the role. So how do mothers cope? The burden of perfection is unbearable. Better to trust that there is a lot they will learn about themselves as they learn about motherhood.

In many tribal societies, it is said that a man proves himself in the hunt or in battle, but a woman proves herself in birthing. Birth and motherhood are extraordinarily challenging and powerful times, offering an unparalleled opportunity for growth and the experience of love. Motherhood is a job for which a woman's only experience is being mothered herself. In a world where family and community support are breaking down, a woman can feel isolated in her new role of provider, carer, nurturer and teacher. The responsibility is awesome, and an easy precursor to feelings of guilt and anxiety, especially when society has as much to say about mothering as it currently does. As women combine professional careers with their roles as mothers and carers, things have become even more complicated. Whether a woman fantasizes about herself as a nurturing Mother Earth figure or a have-it-all Supermum, she will be bombarded by newspapers, magazines and books telling her how many kids to have, how to raise them, where to school them and so on. By manipulating the role of motherhood, the media can manipulate the mother. And such manipulation is often the enemy of self-esteem.

Sheila Kitzinger, a leading exponent of childbirth and healthcare, has said, 'You will find that your baby soon teaches you what to do and will leave you in no doubt about what she likes, when she needs to be fed, played with and talked to, and exactly what makes her feel comfortable and contented. You do not have to rely on 'maternal instincts' for that. They are already there.'

As her child is lifted onto her body, the bonding of mother and child outside the womb begins. The period immediately after the birth is a time of recovery and readjustment to living together as a family. Many partnerships find a new sense of connection. In other partnerships, the new child puts tremendous pressure on the relationship as the mother turns her love away from her partner to her new-born.

'I fell in love the moment I looked into my child's eyes. This little boy became the most important thing in my life. I only realized that something was going wrong with my marriage when my husband went out and bought himself some expensive designer underwear and took to walking around the house with nothing else on,' laughs one recent new mother. 'I got the hint and we spent some time together rekindling our sexual and emotional relationship. I knew I had to share this love with both men in my life. I also realized how much I was missing the love and affection he showered on me during my pregnancy.'

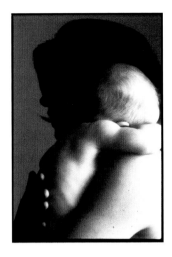

Nothing prepares a woman for the stamina she requires in the early months or the emotional extremes she experiences as she moves from exhaustion, depression and hysteria to joy and love. Anger, aggression, sadness and grief are natural responses in the post-natal period but without the support of other women, a young mother may feel isolated and self-esteem drops to rock bottom. The ability to cope physically and psychologically returns in time.

But these are also days for the mother to be alone with her child, so that she is able to listen to the rhythms of her body and the needs of her baby. Staying in pace with the baby's rhythms can help a mother gently back into life's mainstream. Just as massage, touch, talking and singing to the child make her feel safe and wanted as she is introduced to the family, the mother also needs to be massaged, bathed and cared for. A first-time mother remembers how her elder sister who had three children always said that her favourite gift after giving birth to her eldest child was their mother turning up each evening to cook the family supper. Another woman had a best friend arrange for her masseuse to turn up every two days for a week to give her a body massage. It is valuable for mothers of young children to keep sacred time for themselves either by meditating, walking in nature, reading, sleeping or having lunch with a friend so that they can connect with their own needs.

The roles of motherhood have changed as they adapt to larger extended families due to more divorces and remarriages, single parenthood, and more women working while maintaining their roles as mothers and carers. Fathers are asked to take more responsibility for the upbringing of their children. Shared parenting, either within the family or in a communal living situation, relieves a great deal of pressure from the mother, benefits the child and enables the parents to enjoy periods of solitude and participation in the child's growth, education, creative interests and spiritual teachings.

If infancy is an adventure for children, it is no less so for parents. During those early years the child becomes aware of the family's hobbies and interests, lifestyles and attitudes. This is the first level of education for our children. Rules and habits are the first ways in which the child begins to understand the wider world:

mealtimes, bedtimes, storytelling, painting, playing, television and computer games as well as the negative patterns of family rows, violence, alcoholism, drug-taking, violence, and abandonment or over-discipline. These all establish guidelines for the child. The times of transition for the child also represent the different stages of motherhood: the pre-school years when a mother may leave the workplace to focus on her child; the relative calm of school years when she may return to her professional career; the turbulence of teenage years when the mother is rediscovering her creative identity and her child is moving out into the world; and finally the coming of age, as the child prepares to leave home and the mother enters menopause, another period of transition.

Your Children are not your children.

They are the sons and daughters of Life's longing for itself.

They come through you but not from you,

And though they are with you yet they belong not to you.

You may give them your love but not your thoughts,

For they have their own thoughts.

You may house their bodies but not their soul,

For their souls dwell in the house of tomorrow,

Which you cannot visit, not even in your dreams.

From *The Prophet*, Kahlil Gibran

Puberty and menopause: times of transition

There is an invisible umbilical link between puberty and menopause, the two great transitional phases in a woman's life. The beginning and the end of the menstrual flow encompass a great circle of experience which includes lovers, marriage, divorce, birthing and parenting, professional careers and creative expression. Though they are at opposite ends of the chronological spectrum – one marking the onset of fertility, the other the end of reproductive life – they are nonetheless very similar journeys, a compatability that is recognized in the rituals of those tribal cultures where the initiation of a young girl at the onset of her first period is usually carried out by older women who are entering their menopause. Alice Walker describes the mother-daughter relationship in her book *The Same River Twice*: 'I think mothers and daughters are meant to give birth to each other, over and over. That is why our challenges to each other are so fierce; that is why ... the teaching and learning one from the other is so indelible and bittersweet.'

As daughters and mothers generally enter puberty and menopause at precisely the same moment, this is when those challenges are most acute. Both are times of transformation which involve loss as well as gain. Many ancient myths describe a descent into darkness which a female figure undertakes in order to find what is missing in herself as a woman. Both puberty and menopause involve such a journey when women are forced, often in some confusion and solitude, to look within themselves to find the insight, strength and self-knowledge that will inform the next phase of life. Both are gateways to greater power and freedom, but the transitions are painful.

Most of the emotional and physical fluctuations of both puberty and menopause are fed by the hormonal imbalance caused by dramatic changes in levels of the production of oestrogen. Fitful or heavy periods, emotional highs and lows, aching, and increased pain and loss of concentration are some of the symptoms that women suffer when, as teenagers they acclimatize to the hormone and, as older women withdraw from it.

In contemporary culture, the sharing of information, off-loading burdens and comparing stories remain an integral part of women's support systems. However, at the moment when women most need each other – at puberty and menopause – intergenerational support often breaks down. There are many reasons why. Society places much more pressure on both adolescent and menopausal women. Professional lives and later childbearing mean that many women enter menopause when they are reaching the peak of their career and have young children still at home. The demands on their time and energy are often further stretched by increasingly frail and dependent parents. Meanwhile, women are entering puberty far earlier than our recent ancestors. The average age for girls to encounter menarche in 1877 was nearly fifteen. Today it is nearer twelve. The development of breasts, hips, and hormonal fluctuations begin as early as nine or ten when girls are less emotionally and mentally prepared for such changes.

'One minute I was fine and the next I was in floods of tears. I didn't know what was wrong with me. I was losing control and there was no one that I could talk to about it.'

Finally, as they try to find a sense of their own equilibrium out of the chaos into which they feel they have fallen, both generations are confronting the changes to their bodies surrounded by powerful media images of what it is to be beautiful or sexy. Instead of understanding each other, they become competitive.

It is difficult for older women, and mothers especially, to recognize that their own conflicting ideas about their body are reflected in younger women. However, if menopausal women are engaged in a battle with their own bodies, it is hard to convey positive messages to younger women. In a culture which almost always equates power and sexuality with youth and beauty it becomes almost impossible for women to age without losing a valuable sense of self-esteem, and that has, in turn, fed a huge industry that is dedicated to extending the appearance of youth for as long as possible.

Contrast attitudes in the black community, where women suffer the negative aspects of menopause far less than their white counterparts. Influenced by a matrilineal upbringing, black women enter middle age with enhanced prestige and status. Their sexuality is fed not by how they look but by their spirituality and the esteem which they feel is their entitlement as they reach middle age. Menopause is more readily accepted – even welcomed – as an integral part of life.

A new generation of women entering menopause is challenging prevailing attitudes by looking to alternative treatments: homeopathy, natural supplements, Chinese medicine, ayurvedic practices, yoga, t'ai chi and meditation. Kachina Kutenai, a nurse, teacher and counsellor who works with ancient Apache healing traditions, recommends herbs such as red sage, dandelion and elderberry, supplements of vitamin E, calcium and magnesium, valerian root and Siberian ginseng. She admits that a herbal regime won't work for all women but she is convinced that by listening to and trusting their own bodies, women will emerge from menopause with a much stronger sense of who they are and how powerful they can be.

As teenagers look outward for their new identity, many older women look inward. Instead of seeing menopause solely as the end of youth and fertility, it becomes another initiation – a journey of discovery when women realize that, far from losing strength, they are gaining new stability and, far from being forced to give up their desires, they are able to follow them with more freedom, humour and vision. Their awareness of mortality sparks an exploration of the world of the spirit. For the first time they are able to see themselves quite apart from their beauty or reproductive role and begin to explore their own needs. Many women experience a new awareness of their creative and psychic powers. They find that the new paths open to them become as varied and exciting as they were at adolescence, but now the choices benefit from wisdom and experience.

'When I stopped trying to fight it, I began to see my menopause as a great gift. It presented me with an opportunity to completely re-evaluate my purpose in life. I decided to embrace the changes and trust my instincts. In many ways, it was a real liberation for me.'

It's that wisdom and experience which are such valuable gifts to the generations that follow. Instead of the competitiveness which all too readily springs from the confusion of transition, imagine a cross-generational compatibility, where mothers are able to encourage and empower their daughters' intellectual and sexual identity as they reach towards the freedoms and responsibilities of womanhood; where they can help the younger women to see that they are beautiful as they are, that their bodies are incredible, life-giving vessels which deserve looking after and that, when youth and the duties of motherhood are over, the horizons of fulfilment grow even wider.

The age of the elder

At elderhood, women have reached the final cycle on the wheel of life. It is time for spiritual focus, creative expression and release. It is also the time when the body begins to decline and thoughts turn to the journey of the soul and the passage of death. In Aboriginal and Native American traditions, a woman is recognized as an elder at the age of fifty-six when the planet Saturn reaches its final cycle. Today, due to longer lifespans and healthier lifestyles, a woman usually enters elderhood in her late sixties. This is her gateway to wisdom, acceptance and a deeper understanding of life.

In the past, and within some cultures today, the grandmother, or elder woman, was greatly respected. The lodges or places where they gathered were important for the political and social structure of the tribe as their knowledge, gained from their journey through life, was widely sought after. They were wise women, healers and midwives, and people came to them for advice on relationships, families, health and motherhood. Today, particularly in the West, old women are often left feeling ignored and useless, due to the breakdown of family and community life and the fear of death and ageing. In losing respect for their wisdom and perspective, our society loses the immeasurable gifts of knowledge and experience. Allegra Taylor, a writer, healer and mother of six children, was determined to celebrate her grandmotherhood. She celebrated the death of the old and the birth of the new for her new grandchild's other grandmother and three female friends.

'For us as much as for the baby it was a rite of passage. We each held the tiny girl in our arms and kissed her and blessed her. It was a time of great love and tenderness – infinitely potent. We had reclaimed something of incalculable value – the collective power of the older woman. It was the most beautiful feeling of continuation, of having an active, useful, unique role to play in letting go of the last phase of our lives and moving proudly and vitally into the next.'

Throughout the developing world the role of the grandmother remains a vital one for, as the mother and father go out to work, they will often leave their children with their parents. Even in our culture the relationship between grandparent and grandchild is unique and tender as their love is less conditional on time and tasks, discipline and personality struggles. The sense of continuity brings valuable perspective to the rest of the family. Personal memories and stories are part of a living history and are often a source of stability for both individual families and the wider community.

The journey into old age is not an easy one. Frailty of the body and the encroaching awareness of death are frightening realities. Difficulties in mobility and communication can come as a great shock to a normal healthy woman and bring fears of 'becoming a burden'. But as normal activity becomes impossible and everyday tasks become more and more difficult, an appreciation of the simple pleasures creeps into daily life. The frailties which we suffer as we approach death are simply part of the process of letting go. Our bodies are helping us to relinquish life in its physical form. As time slows to a more measured pace, the mind is able to turn more easily to the concerns of the spirit.

'Old age is surely a time to learn about magic, about healing powers, divination and prophecy,' writes Allegra Taylor. 'A time to walk the mystical path with practical feet.'

The slow process of letting go, as emotional and physical connections to life weaken and loved ones die, may last many years. It may be frightening at first but eventually it becomes part of the understanding of the natural cycle of life and death and the possibilities of transformation. Women who have lost their trust in the processes of old age and hold a great deal of anger, resentment or bitterness about their lives may find a new spiritual identity. Death loses its dread and allows the elder to embrace the remaining days of her life with passion and joy.

One woman's experience

Corrie Gray was forty-two when her first husband and the much-loved father of her three children suffered a massive heart attack. For months he remained in hospital while doctors carried out a battery of tests. 'They refused to tell us what was going on and finally told me how sick he was four days before he died. When I asked what I should tell my children they said, "Nothing – you will need all your strength yourself."

'So he died at four o'clock in the morning on a ventilator attached to tubes and drips in intensive care. No one was with him and the doctors advised me against bringing the children to see him. The doctors prescribed valium for me and sent me home. I popped pills for the next six months so I was completely out of it and unable to mourn. There was no one to talk to, no counselling. My parents put away all our wedding photographs and stopped mentioning his name. I just hoped that it would be better after a year but it never was.'

When her second husband was diagnosed with terminal cancer, Corrie was determined that they would meet his death in a completely different way from that of her first husband.

'I made sure that I received support and advice from the people and professionals around me. I wanted to support him on every phase of his journey and I made sure that his children were involved. He was determined that he was not going to die; we tried diets, went to doctors and clinics as he refused to accept the initial prognosis. His great strength gave us time to take it all in and spend precious time with him as his life force ebbed away. When finally he lay dying, there was deep sadness but also enormous love as he slipped in and out of consciousness. When he died, a tremendous sense of peace and spirit came into the room. There were no pills to deaden the pain this time. I felt the full shock of sadness and loneliness. I spent some time alone with him and after breaking down, I was finally able to let him go and wish him well on his journey.'

The final rite of passage

Women were the traditional guardians of the cycles of life. Birth and death were their domain. They would tend the sick and help prepare them for their death, be with them on their vigil and hold them as they took their last breath. Then they would take care of the body and lead loved ones in mourning. Their knowledge and experience was passed from generation to generation.

Today, the drama of death is played out in hospitals and clinics, its mysteries the province of doctors and science. Our lack of familiarity with death means that we cannot know how to deal with it. It is alienating. Even though attitudes to death and dying have evolved in recent years, with the popularization of Buddhism, Eastern mysticism and tribal cultures, the idea that death is a point of celebration in the cycle of life needs to be more understood in the Western world. We need to break down the taboo surrounding it and learn to understand it as a necessary part of the everlasting cycle of life and regeneration instead of trying to control it through our fear. After all, if we could fully understand the final mystery, we might gain real insight into the transformative nature of the soul as it touches birth, life, love, suffering and, finally, death on its spiritual journey through infinity.

In less industrialized countries, where community and tradition still hold more power than science and medicine, death remains one of the most important moments where people gather to mourn and celebrate. Life is suspended, sometimes for weeks at a time, as elaborate rituals are carried out or people are simply allowed to take time out to grieve. The acknowledgement by the whole community of a death in any family soothes their suffering and helps them make sense of their loss.

This response suggests an appreciation of the fact that the dying bring great gifts to the people around them. It is rare that we come so close to mortality. It helps us to see the relative importance of other issues in our lives, and the courage, humour or wisdom that the dying show can be a great inspiration. We also begin to examine our own beliefs about death. Whatever our religious conviction, it is rare that the death of a loved one does not instil in us a personal belief in immortality. But the space that a death creates can feel like a huge void. At this time, outward expressions of grief, sadness and a celebration of the life passed are healthy and help the living, especially children, to fully experience their loss and release the pain of loss.

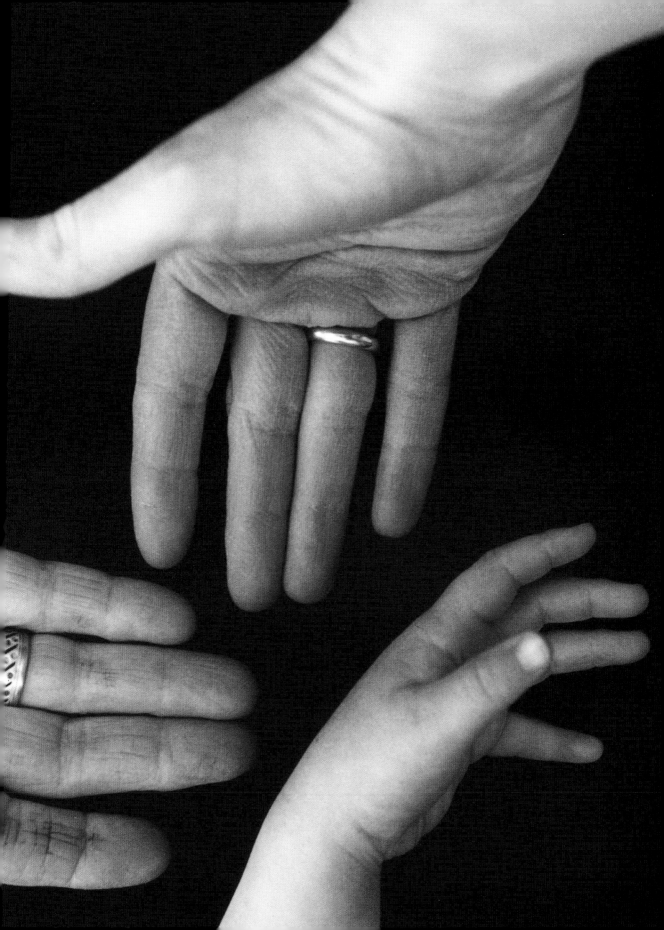

Useful addresses

The Body Shop International plc
Watersmead
Littlehampton
West Sussex BN17 6LS
tel: (020) 7208 7600
fax: (01903) 726250
email: info@bodyshop.co.uk
http://www.the-body-shop.com

ACUPUNCTURE

British Acupuncture Council
Park House
206-8 Latimer Road
London W10 6RE
tel: (020) 8964 0222

Australian Acupuncture Association Ltd and Acupuncture and Ethics Standards Organisation
PO Box 5142
West End
Queensland 4101

Acupuncture Association of Victoria
1 Gordon Street
Moorabbin
Victoria 3189
tel: (03) 9557 6100

The Australian Medical Acupuncture Society
5 Lord Street
Roseville
New South Wales 2069
tel: (02) 9415 6800

ALEXANDER TECHNIQUE

Society of Teachers of the Alexander Technique
20 London House
266 Fulham Road
London SW10 9EL
tel: (020) 7351 0828
(for further information please send an A5 stamped addressed envelope with a 31p stamp)

Australian Society of Alexander Technique (AUSTAT)
Liverpool Street
Sydney 2000

Australian Society of the Teachers of the Alexander Technique
16 Princess Street
Kew
Victoria 3101
tel: (03) 9853 1356

AROMATHERAPY

Aromatherapy Trade Council
PO Box 52
Market Harborough
Leicestershire LE16 8ZX
tel/fax: (01858) 465731

Aromatherapy Organisations Council
PO Box 355
Croydon CR9 2QP
tel: (020) 8251 7912

International Federation of Aromatherapists
Bellevue Hill
New South Wales 2023

Aromatherapy Clinic of Sydney
1 O'Connell Street
Sydney
New South Wales 2000
tel: (02) 9241 4030

ART THERAPY

British Association of Art Therapists
11a Richmond Road
Brighton BN2 3RL

AUTOGENICS

British Association for Autogenic Training and Therapy
c/o The Royal London Homeopathic Hospital NHS Trust
Great Ormond Street
London WC1N 3HR
(for further information please send a stamped addressed envelope)

AYURVEDA

Ayurvedic Medical Association UK
59 Dulverton Road
Selsdon
Croydon CR2 8PJ

Maharishi Ayurveda
579 Punt Road
South Yarra
Victoria 3141
tel: (03) 9866 1999

BIOFEEDBACK

Ultramind Ltd
2 Lindsey Street
London EC1A 9HP
(for details about equipment and
interactive software for home use)

BOWEN TECHNIQUE

Bowtech
38 Portway
Frome
Somerset BA11 5EN
tel/fax: (01373) 461873
email: bowen@globalnet.co.uk
http://www.bowtechUK.com

CHIROPRACTIC

**British Chiropractic
Association**
Blagrave House
17 Blagrave Street
Reading RG1 1QB
tel: (0118) 950 5950

**Chiropractors' Association of
Australia**
3 Wood Street
Ashfield
New South Wales 2131

**Chiropractors' Association of
Australia**
National Head Quarters
459 Great Western Highway
Falconbridge
New South Wales 2776
tel: (02) 4751 5644

**Chiropractors' Association of
Victoria**
319 Victoria Road
Brunswick
Victoria 3056
tel: (03) 9387 9377

CLIMBING

**British Mountaineering
Council**
177-79 Burton Road
Manchester M20 2BB
tel: (0161) 445 4747
email: office@thebmc.co.uk
http://www.thebmc.co.uk

CRANIO-SACRAL THERAPY

The Upledger Institute UK
52 Main Street
Perth PH2 8AH
tel: (01738) 444404

HEALING

Wentworth Street Clinic
Level 3
39 East Esplanade
Manly
New South Wales 2095
tel: (02) 9977 0144

HELLERWORK/ROLFING

Bodyworkers
Suite 211
Coppergate House
16 Brune Street
London E1 7NJ

PO Box 14793
London SW1V 2WB

HERBALISM

**Register of Chinese Herbal
Medicine (RCHM)**
PO Box 400
Wembley
Middlesex HA9 9NZ
tel: (07000) 790332
fax: (020) 7377 8553
(for a list of local practioners
please send an A5 stamped
addressed envelope and a cheque
or postal order for £2.50)

**National Institute of Medical
Herbalists**
56 Longbrook Street
Exeter
Devon EX4 6AH

**National Herbalists
Association of Australia**
305/3 Small Street
Broadway
New South Wales 2001

HOMEOPATHY

**British Homeopathic
Association**
27a Devonshire Street
London W1N 1RJ

**Australian Homeopathic
Association**
PO Box 82
Gladesville
New South Wales 2111

**Australian Federation of
Homeopaths**
238 Ballarat Road
Footscray
Victoria 3011
tel: (03) 9318 3057

Useful addresses

HYPNOTHERAPY

British Society of Experimental and Clinical Hypnosis
c/o Phyllis Alden
Department of Psychology
Grimsby General Hospital
Scartho Road
Grimsby
South Humberside DN33 2BA

National Register of Hypnotherapists and Psychotherapists
National College of Hypnosis
and Psychotherapy
12 Cross Street
Nelson
Lancashire BB9 7EN

Australian Society of Clinical Hypnotherapists
38 Denistone Road
Eastwood
New South Wales 2122

IRIDOLOGY

International Association of Clinical Iridologists
Orchards Villa
Porters Park Drive
Shenley
Hertfordshire WD7 9DS
tel: (01923) 850 5588
fax: (01923) 857670
email: inso@taylor-jackson.com
http://www.taylor-jackson.com

KARATE

English Karate Governing Body
tel: (01225) 834008

KENDO

British Kendo Association
tel: (020) 7515 8653

KINESIOLOGY

International College of Applied Kinesiology UK
Downsview
New Hall Lane
Small Dole
West Sussex BN5 9YI
(for register of trained practitioners)

Kinesiology Foundation
PO Box 83
Sheffield S7 2YN

Australian Kinesiology Association
PO Box 88
Ormond
Victoria 3204
tel: (03) 9578 9322

MASSAGE

British Massage Therapy Council (BMTC)
Greenbank House
65a Adelphi Street
Preston
Lancashire PR1 7BH
tel/fax: (01722) 881063

Associated of Remedial Masseurs Inc
120 Blaxland Road
Ryde
New South Wales 2118

Association of Massage Therapists
Level 1
47 Spring Street
Bondi Junction
New South Wales 2022
tel: (02) 9369 2998

Association of Massage Therapists of Victoria
250 High Street
Prahan
Victoria 3181
tel: (03) 9510 3030

MEDITATION

Friends of the Western Buddhist Order
London Buddhist Centre
51 Roman Road
London E2 0HU

Freepost
London SW1P 4YY
(for details on transcendental meditation)

METAMORPHIC TECNHIQUE

UK Metamorphic Association
67 Ritherdon Road
Tooting
London SW17 8QE

MUSIC THERAPY

Association of Professional Music Therapists
Chestnut Cottage
38 Pierce Lane
Fulbourn
Cambridge CB1 5DL

OSTEOPATHY

Osteopathic Information Service (OIS)
Premier House
10 Greycoat Place
London SW1P 1SB
tel: (020) 7799 2559

Australian Osteopathic Association
PO Box 699
Turramurra
New South Wales 2074
tel: (02) 9449 4799

POLARITY THERAPY

Federation of Polarity Trainings
7 Nunney Close
Golden Valley
Cheltenham GL51 0TU

PSYCHOTHERAPY AND COUNSELLING

UK Council for Psychotherapy
167-69 Great Portland Street
London W1N 5FB

Australian and New Zealand Society of Jungian Analysts, Analysis and Psychotherapy
PO Box 190
Paddington
New South Wales 2021

REFLEXOLOGY

Australian Association of Reflexology
9 Steward Avenue
Matraville
New South Wales 2056
tel: (02) 9311 2322

REIKI

The Reiki Association
Cornbrook Bridge Road
Cornbrook
Clee Hill
Ludlow
Shropshire SY8 3QQ
tel: (01981) 550829
fax: (01584) 891197
email: KateReikiJones@
compuserve.com

SHAMANISM

The Sacred Trust
PO Box 603
Bath BA1 2ZU
tel: (01225) 852615
email: sacredtrust@
compuserve.com

SHIATSU

Shiatsu Society of the UK
Suite B
Barber House
Storey's Bar Road
Fengate
Peterborough PE1 5YN
tel: (01733) 758341
fax: (01733) 758342
(for a list of local registered practitioners please send a stamped addressed envelope)

Shiatsu Therapy Association
332 Carlisle Street
Bataclava
Victoria 3186
tel (03) 9752 6711

T'AI CHI

T'ai Chi Union for Great Britain
23 Oakwood Avenue
Mitcham
Surrey CR4 3DQ

UK T'ai Chi Association
PO Box 159
Bromley BR1 3XX

YOGA

British Wheel of Yoga
1 Hamilton Place
Boston Road
Sleaford
Lincolnshire NG34 7ES
tel: (01529) 306851
(for a list of practitioners please send an A5 stamped addressed envelope)

International Yoga Teachers Association
PO Box 207
St Ives
New South Wales 2975

Australian Yoga Masters Association
183 Pitt Town Road
Kenthurst
New South Wales 2156
tel: (02) 9564 9030

ZERO BALANCING

Zero Balancing Association UK
10 Victoria Grove
Bridport
Dorset DT6 3AA
tel: (01308) 420007
email: zbauk@aol.com

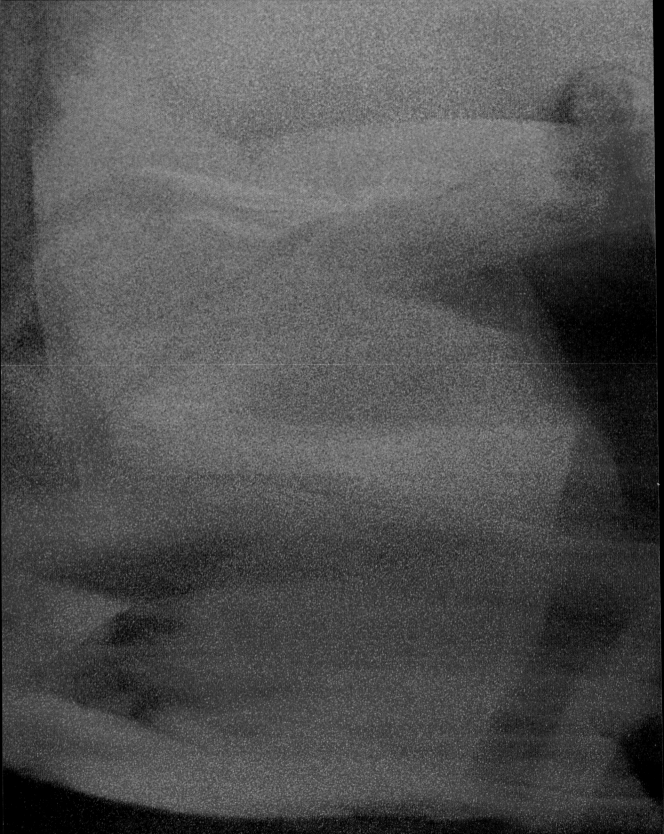

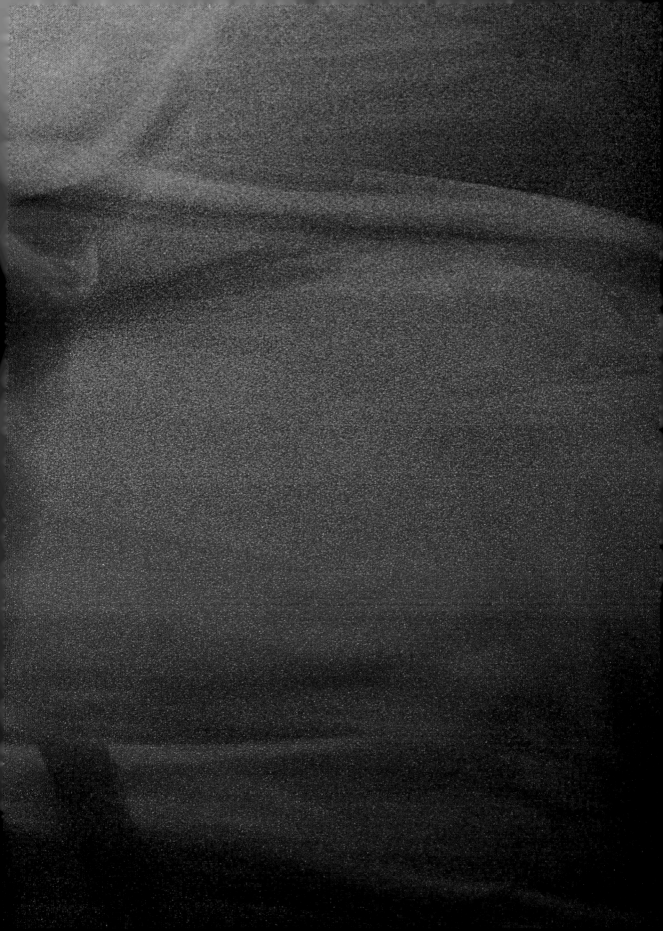

About the writers

WELLBEING AND THE MIND-BODY CONNECTION

Tim Blanks has worked for The Body Shop for eight years as an in-house editor and copywriter. He wrote for and edited *The Body Shop Book* in 1994, and is also host of the internationally syndicated television magazine show *Fashion File*. (Fax: 020 7436 7166)

WELLBEING AND INTERNAL FITNESS

Simon Brown is a registered shiatsu and feng shui practitioner, and has published books on both subjects. As a full-time feng shui consultant he lectures internationally and his clients range from celebrities such as Boy George to companies such as British Airways and The Body Shop. He has also trained in macrobiotics. (Tel/fax: 020 7431 9897)

WELLBEING AND EXERCISE

Bronwyn Cosgrave is currently commissioning editor for *Vogue*. She has written on fashion, fitness, beauty and health for everything from *The Sunday Times* to *Paris Vogue*. She is also the fashion historian for *Encyclopaedia Britannica*. (Tel: 020 7352 2550)

WELLBEING AND THE WAY YOU LOOK

Jennifer Wood worked for nine years as a writer for The Body Shop. She now freelances on a wide range of subjects. (Tel/fax: 020 8892 2999)

WELLBEING AND THE POWER OF TOUCH

Vicci Bentley is a health and beauty expert with 25 years' experience. She is a trained reiki practitioner. (Tel: 020 8998 3325)

FOOD FOR THE SOUL AND WELLBEING AND THE SOUL

Natalia O'Sullivan is a holistic writer for magazines and newspapers. A trained therapist with shiatsu, reflexology, and aromatherapy skills, she specializes in treating women, pregnant mothers and menopausal women for emotional, physical and spiritual conditions, and facilitates retreats and workshops around the world on sacred and shamanic healing, with particular emphasis on the Celtic traditions of Scotland, Ireland and Wales. (Tel: 01278 653142; fax: 01278 653771)

Nicola Graydon is a London-based freelance writer and photographer for newspapers and magazines, including *The Evening Standard* and *Harpers and Queen*. Her specialties are women's issues and the environment. She has travelled widely throughout Africa researching tribal culture. She studies hatha yoga and shamanic teaching. (Tel/fax: 020 7603 6435)

Index

Acknowledgments

The publisher thanks the photographers and organizations for their kind permission to reproduce the following photographs in this book:

pages 6-7 Photonica / Nicholas Pavloff; 10 Tony Stone Images / PT Santana; 13 left Body Shop International / Carol Beckwith; 13 centre Body Shop International / Thomas L Kelly; 13 right Body Shop International / Carol Beckwith; 14 Body Shop International / Eric Richmond; 16 Attard Photolibrary; 19 Marie France / Marc Montezin / Dominique Eveque; 20-21 Body Shop International / Eric Richmond; 23 Photonica / Barnaby Hall; 35 Getty Images / Keith Brotsky; 36 Body Shop International / Eric Richmond; 38 Attard Photolibrary; 43 Photonica / Tadashi Osumi; 45 Attard Photolibrary; 47 Science Photo Library / BSIP Ducloux; 48 Attard Photolibrary; 49 Photonica / David Perry; 50 Tim Evans Cook; 53 Attard Photolibrary; 54 Attard Photolibrary; 56 Robert Harding Picture Library / Roger Stowell; 57 Attard Photolibrary; 59 Photonica / F Engelhorn; 62 Ebury Press / Sandra Lane; 66 Attard Photolibrary; 71 Getty Images / Darryl Torckler; 72-73 Marie France / Alois Boer / Dominique Eveque; 74 Robert Harding Picture Library / Bildagentur Schuster; 78 Photonica / R Nakagawa; 80 Getty Images / David Stewart; 83 Photonica / Y Hirota; 85 above Jonathan Root; 85 centre above Jonathan Root; 85 centre below Jonathan Root; 85 below Jonathan Root; 87 above left Jonathan Root; 87 below left Jonathan Root; 87 above right Jonathan Root; 87 below right Jonathan Root; 89 Getty Images / Lori Adamski Peak; 90 Getty Images / Lori Adamski Peak; 92 Special Photographers' Library / Polly Sansome; 93 Getty Images / David Madison; 96 Photonica / Tim Pannell; 97 Getty Images / Dave Rosenberg; 101 Photonica / Mia Klien; 102 Getty Images / Bruce Ayers; 103 The Image Bank / T Stableford; 105 Photonica / James Gritz; 106-107 Photonica / Hitomi Okada; 108 Body Shop International / Eric Richmond; 113 Body Shop International / Eric Richmond; 115 Body Shop International / Matt Shave; 121 Body Shop International / Matt Shave; 122 Attard Photolibrary; 125 left Jonathan Root; 125 centre Jonathan Root; 125 right Jonathan Root; 127 Body Shop International / Eric Richmond; 128 Getty Images / Phil Borges; 129 Photonica / Jay Corbett; 130 Jonathan Root; 131 Jonathan Root; 132 Jonathan Root; 133 Getty Images / Mark Harwood; 136 The Image Bank / P Porcella; 138 Getty Images / Christopher Bissell; 140 The Image Bank / Juan Silva; 145 Photonica / Gentl & Hyers; 146 Photonica / Robin M White; 150 Millennium / Tansy Spinks; 152 Photonica / Doug Plummer; 153 Attard Photolibrary; 154 Getty Images / Andrew Hall; 155 The Image Bank / Wayne H Chasan; 157 The Image Bank / Philip Porcella; 159 Jonathan Root; 162 Jonathan Root; 164 Jonathan Root; 171 Jonathan Root; 175 Jean-Loup Charmet; 176 Ebury Press / Marie-Louise Avery; 177 Getty Images / Kevin Morris; 178 Science Photo Library / Martin Dohrn; 182 above Body Shop International / Matt Shave; 182 below Body Shop International / Matt Shave; 185 below Body Shop International / Matt Shave; 185 above Body Shop International / Matt Shave; 186 Body Shop International / Max Jourdan; 187 Body Shop International / Max Jourdan; 188 Body Shop International / Matt Shave; 193 Ebury Press / Sandra Lane; 194 Body Shop International / Eric Richmond; 196 Garden Picture Library / Ute Klaphake; 198 Getty Images / Chris Windsor; 202-203 The Image Bank / Nicolas Russell; 206 Getty Images / James Darell; 212 Getty Images / Jean-Francois Gate; 214 Elizabeth Whiting Associates / Fabienne Catherine; 218 Photonica / N Sutherland; 224 Getty Images / Laurence Monneret; 227 Collections / Anthea Sieveking; 229 Collections / Sandra Lousada; 230 The Special Photographers' Library / Caroline Molloy; 232 Getty Images / Carol Ford; 236 The Image Bank / Yan Kang Yong; 241 Millennium / Tansy Spinks; 242-243 Getty Images / Chad Ehlers; 248-249 Photonica / Paul Vordic.

The publisher also thanks The Women's Press for allowing publication of the extract taken from Alice Walker's *The Same River Twice* that appears on page 233.